POETRY COMPETITION
FOR 11-18 YEAR-OLDS

GW00692303

Co Antrim
Edited by Jessica Woodbridge

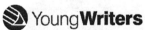 Young**Writers**

First published in Great Britain in 2006 by:
Young Writers
Remus House
Coltsfoot Drive
Peterborough
PE2 9JX
Telephone: 01733 890066
Website: www.youngwriters.co.uk

SB ISBN 1 84602 372 6

Foreword

This year, the Young Writers' *POP! - The Power Of Poetry* competition proudly presents a showcase of the best poetic talent selected from thousands of up-and-coming writers nationwide.

Young Writers was established in 1991 to promote the reading and writing of poetry within schools and to the young of today. Our books nurture and inspire confidence in the ability of young writers and provide a snapshot of poems written in schools and at home by budding poets of the future.

The thought, effort, imagination and hard work put into each poem impressed us all and the task of selecting poems was a difficult but nevertheless enjoyable experience.

We hope you are as pleased as we are with the final selection and that you and your family continue to be entertained with *POP! Co Antrim* for many years to come.

Contents

Elizabeth Cartwright (12)	43
Gareth Gould (11)	43
Ryan Richardson (11)	44
Karl Morris (12)	44
Zara Morrow (11)	45
Ashley Knapper (13)	45
Rachel Walker (12)	46
James Woolsey (11)	46
Ryan Peacock (11)	47
Robyn Foster (12)	47
Helen Peden (12)	48
Alannah Stirling (11)	48
James Hyde (12)	49
Patrick Lecky (12)	49
Hayley Carole Donaldson (12)	50
Rebecca Steele (11)	50
Jake Smith (11)	51
Kerri Moore (11)	52
Rebecca Docherty (12)	52
Natalie Parke (11)	53
Judith Patterson (11)	53
Victoria Howarth (12)	54
Anna Gardiner (11)	55
Lauren Patton (12)	55
Gareth Holden (12)	56
Laura Dempster (12)	56
Hannah Fletcher (11)	57
Paul Duncan (11)	57
Chael McLean (13)	58
Malin Murphy (12)	58
Catherine Gawn (11)	59
Katherine Gould (11)	59
Andrew Patterson (12)	60
Timothy Woolsey (12)	60
Debbie Quigley (12)	60
Emma McFadden (14)	61
Mark Lewis (13)	61
Amy Adams (12)	62
Emma Osborne (12)	63
James Fulton (11)	63
Jack Parte (12)	64
Ben Lewis (12)	64

Liam Hind (13)	65
David Brown (12)	65

Ballyclare High School

Martha Watson (14)	66
Sam Burnison (15)	66
Dawn Comins (14)	67
Ryan Cooke (14)	68
Stuart Greer (14)	68
Simon Mees (14)	69
Lauren Magowan (13)	70
Kirsty Johnston (15)	70
Chris Grimley (14)	71
Joanna Davis (14)	71
Kyle Crawford (13)	72
Sarah-Jane Montgomery (13)	73
Laura French (16)	74
Michael Morrison (15)	74
Mark Wilson (16)	75
Robyn Patton (12)	75
Ross Glover (13)	76
Andrew McCunn (14)	76
Daniel Barnett (13)	77
Rachael Stronge (15)	77
Matthew Jackson (14)	78
Rachel McNeilly (14)	79
Ian Moxen (12)	80
Connor Gilpin (13)	80
David McDowell (13)	81
Chris Bew (13)	81
Jennifer McBrien (13)	82
Stuart McGreevy (13)	83
Matthew McKeown (13)	84
Jonathan Crone (13)	84
Ben Coote (13)	85
Ryan Wallace (13)	85
Mark Gault (13)	86
Devan Brown (11)	86
Rachel McMillan (13)	87
Hannah Welshman (11)	88
Christina Turkington (12)	88

Holly Steele-Nicholson (15)	89
Luke Johnston (12)	90
Orla Carmichael (13)	90
James Hall (11)	91
Alastair Hunter (11)	91
Nicholas Wray (14)	92
Chloe Pickering (11)	92
Hannah Coleman (15)	93
Leah Spiers (11)	93
Amy Lockhart (14)	94
Gareth Armstrong (12)	95
Christopher Davis (12)	95
Ryan Cochrane (13)	96
Andrew Kelly (15)	96
Lauryn Scott (16)	97
Rachel Herron (12)	97
Jane Croskery (13)	98
Louisa Johnston (13)	98
Hannah McClure (12)	99
Zara Taylor (15)	99
Hannah McClay (11)	100
Peter Kennedy (12)	100
James Conville (12)	101
Sarah McConnell (12)	101
Suzanne James (12)	102
Rebecca Bonar (12)	103
Marc Logan (12)	103
Sonia Crawford (13)	104
Mark Rowntree (12)	104
Suzanne Wilson (12)	105
Rebecca Rankin (12)	105
Paul White (13)	106
Ellie Watson (11)	106
Laura Thompson (11)	107
Nicola Lennon (12)	107
Sarah Carmichael (11)	108
Amy McConnell & Catherine Crawford (16)	108
Shauna-Lee Warwick (11)	109
Laura Fekkes (11)	109
Jill Morrow (12)	110
Megan Patterson (13)	110
Sarah Shannon (12)	111

Ballymena Academy

The Poems

Over The Top

I wait there listening for the whistle
My gun loaded and my feet damp,
I feel cold; the winter has brought snow to the trenches.
Once there were puddles of water in the trench
The ground was wet and pleasant to walk on
Now the puddles are frozen, the ground is as hard as concrete.
I hear the whistle and I join my friends in the savage climb over the
trench wall,
I climb over the barbed wire into no-man's-land.
I can hear the enemy guns firing at me -
I think . . . *this is madness.*
I look around and watch my friends slide and slip in the snow,
The red lines of tracer flying between the men in the advance.
Men fall flat on their faces
Others fall and get up and keep going,
I jump into the enemy trenches and join a new war - a war fought
by bayonets.

Calum McGill (13)
Antrim Grammar School

Friends

I think friends are really cool people,
That give and share and always care.
I like people who are really quite friendly,
Who will help me with my homework
And come round for tea.
I think friends are important to have
For they never let you down in awkward situations.
I have a friend called Stephanie Bond,
She's tall and thin and laughs out loud.
Friends can sometimes be really quite strange,
But I still think that friends are really cool people,
That give and share and always care.

Grace Coughlan (12)
Antrim Grammar School

My Dog Bubbles

My dog Bubbles likes playing in puddles,
She really does like getting wet!
My dog Bubbles likes getting cuddles,
She really is a great pet!

My dog Bubbles likes being a pain,
She really is quite annoying sometimes!
My dog Bubbles is quite insane,
She gets up to all sorts of crimes!

My dog Bubbles really likes to cause people grief,
She really likes to mess about all day!
My dog Bubbles really likes destroying things
With her teeth,
She really likes to get her own way!

Louise McClurkin (13)
Antrim Grammar School

Shadow

I stand alone in a darkened alleyway,
Under the blanket of stars above.
No one around to hear my echoed thought,
No one to down my sorrows.

I step out into a city of lights,
People hurrying home.
No one there the same as me
All of them have a family.

I only have one friend at all.
He's always there beside me.
Never leaves my side, does he?
My trusted friend, my shadow.

Amy McIlwaine (13)
Antrim Grammar School

Bodies In The Snow

Thundering bullets soar over my head,
As I try to sleep in my water-logged bed,
Rustling and scurrying of rats and mice,
And the ever present itching of filthy lice.

It'll soon be my turn to 'go over the top',
My only hope's that this war will stop,
Otherwise my end is near,
And this will be my final year.

I suddenly awake to my officer's shout,
'Right lads, it's time to move out!'
I say a final goodbye to my friend,
Because I know this is my end.

Up the bank, out of the trench we go,
First glance of no-man's-land, bodies littering the snow,
We run through them, jumping the barbed wire,
Attempting to dodge the enemies' fire.

My friend is hit, he screams out in pain,
Then more deafening shots are heard again,
I feel a pain, I've been shot I know,
I too join the bodies in the snow.

Rebecca Grant (14)
Antrim Grammar School

This Wasteful War

In all my life
I have never seen
The point of war
In our land so green.
The last farewells
Of fathers and sons
As they meet their death
Through the barrels of guns.

Amy Higginson (14)
Antrim Grammar School

What I Feel For You!

What I feel for you,
Is an emotion so deep,
One which I cannot explain.
You make me feel happy, when I'm sad,
You make me feel joyful even if I feel bad.
What I feel for you is so strong,
So meaningful and true,
I wish you'd feel this way for me too!

What about those memories of me you have?
You brushed them aside,
As if they don't mean a thing!
Did you really mean to
Or was it a stupid mistake?
Will you regret it tomorrow,
And live for today?
Or will the memories just flood away?

Nicola McCleery (13)
Antrim Grammar School

Sleeping

I love to sleep drifting away
At night I sometimes read
And I feel like I'm reading the same line over again,
And I feel like I'm reading the same line over again,
And I feel like I'm reading the same line over again.
Then I put the book down and look out the window
And hear the roaring wind and the pouring rain
Then I feel I'm drifting away.
Then my sister starts crying,
Will I ever sleep? Who knows, I hope I get to go soon -
To the land over the moon, zzzzzzzzzzz
That was a good night's rest.

Clarke Feeney (11)
Antrim Grammar School

Why?

I stand alone in the dark of night,
Looking at the sky,
And wonder why.

Why the stars shine so bright,
Giving out such a wonderful light.

Why the moon stares back at me,
Inspiring dreams of what could be.

Why the planets orbit the sun,
Yet ours seems to be the only living one!

Why do we exist at all?
Why do humans stand so tall?
Above the beasts and birds of the sky,
Our intelligence soars so high!

So why are we all destined to die?

Karen McKnight (14)
Antrim Grammar School

The Best Cake In The World

Lardman rushes to the cake shop wondering what to buy,
'Hmmm,' he thinks, munching his apple, 'Maybe a rhubarb pie.'
'A fine choice, my dear sir!' cries Cecil Kneader
- The mind reader.
So in he goes to the cake shop dancing and prancing around,
Finally he is at home, but what is this, what has he found?
It is magnificent, marvellous, truly divine,
Look at it gleam! Look at it shine!
It is a cake, a brilliant cake,
So he picks it up and dunks it in his 'bake.'

Jake McClay (12)
Antrim Grammar School

My Country Needs Me

This year the Earth is torn by trenches,
Like the scars that tear us every day.
This war may be over for Christmas,
But so may the warriors.

'It is sweet and proper to die for your country'
Fickle may I be but I pray,
A box of ash over a crater any day.

'Your country needs you!' the poster said,
But where is my country when I need her?
She will not be found in a crater,
Nor hanging from the wire.

She is shouting on street corners,
And 'fighting' with feathers,

'Charge boys, charge!'

Colin Hagan (14)
Antrim Grammar School

The Eagle

Large eyes always open,
Roaming confidently,
No one steps in his domain,
For he is keeping sentry.
The king of the skies,
With his piercing eyes.
He rules from a lofty fortress,
He swoops,
He swerves,
He glides,
He curves,
And then -
He strikes from the heavens
On his unsuspecting victims.

Crae Wasson (13)
Antrim Grammar School

Don't Label Me!

There's goths and there's punks
And skater dudes too!
But instead of fitting into the crowd
I'm breaking away from the glue!

I don't want to be an airhead
Or even an intelligent geek
I'm not big or small nor fat or thin
Pretty or ugly, strong or weak!

I just want to be me
With nothing added on
No laid back, no psycho freak
Those little names are like so totally gone!

So now I'm just Carrie
That makes me happy as can be!
'Cause no matter how hard you try
You can't *ever* replace me!

Carrie Ingram (13)
Antrim Grammar School

After The War!

Deep down in the dark of the trenches,
In the muddy hole a long way from civilisation,
I stand next to the dead body of a friend,
I'm surrounded by corpses that look in pain,
Their wounds look like someone took time and
Effort to do them as painfully as they could,
Out in front I can only see burnt out and
Destroyed land, it's completely flat!
The only bumps are bodies, dead bodies!
There's no life left here at all,
What happened?

Becky McAllister (13)
Antrim Grammar School

Leave Me Alone

Put my head down
And walk with speed.
Don't look their way,
Just try to get away.

Can't tell anyone
They'd only find out,
If I just ignore it,
It'll go away on its own.

There are more of them,
Than there is of me -
I can't stand up to them,
I'll just leave it alone.

But if I can't tell anyone,
And if I can't stand up to them.
Then if I just ignore it,
Will they really leave me alone?

Matthew Murray (13)
Antrim Grammar School

Barn Owl

With your beautiful heart-shaped face,
And the softness of your wings,
You outstand the human race,
The most beautiful of all things.

In the barn where you sleep all day,
Mice scurry under your feet,
At night you awake and fly away,
Your wings not emitting a beat.

From your night's hunt you return,
You fly with skill and grace,
So from your smartness we should learn,
You outstand the human race.

Louise McBride (13)
Antrim Grammar School

Boys

Tall, dark and handsome,
Short, pale and gross.
Gucci models and actors,
There's only one I like the most.

He's in my very school
But I will not give his name,
For everyone would tease me
And I couldn't live with the shame.

He's tall, pale and handsome,
With great big puppy-dog eyes,
And when I walk straight past him,
I almost melt inside.

Even though he's older,
My friends all think he's lame.
These comments really hurt me
But I like him all the same.

Rachel Smith (13)
Antrim Grammar School

Dinosaurs

D igging up their bones
 I n the dark, dirty soil
N ever before have we seen them
O ver ten feet high!
 S eeing them would make you stare
A t their big ferocious teeth
U nder the blazing sun
R aking in their victims
    With their big, sharp claws.

Matthew Turner (12)
Antrim Grammar School

The Seasons

The spring is when the birds fly home,
They build their nests on their own,
Then they swoop to catch their prey
Until the winter this is where they'll stay.

The summer is the hottest season of the year
That's when we know the holidays are here.
June, July, August and September,
Summer's the season I'll always remember.

The autumn is when the leaves fall down
The trees are bare, the leaves are brown,
This is when it starts to get colder,
2005 is soon getting older.

Winter is when it starts to snow
And excitement for Christmas begins to grow
Piles of presents under the tree
Waiting there for you and me.

Jenny McKeown (13)
Antrim Grammar School

The Lion

It lies in the long grass,
Waiting for its prey,
When in the distance,
There it was,
He got closer and closer,
Trying not to make a sound,
Closer, closer, closer he got,
And then when the antelope turned its back,
He pounced.
One swipe with the claw,
And a long bite in the throat.
There the lion lay,
Proud as could be, ripping the antelope apart.

Jonny Minford (12)
Antrim Grammar School

When Will We Learn?

Is violence really the best answer?
Is war really the only way?
How long must the fighting go on for?
How many people must we slay?

Will they ever quit the terror?
Will there ever be peace?
Is it really a religious war?
Is it ever going to cease?

Why can this world not support us all?
Why must some live in poverty?
When will we learn to help each other?
When will there be equality?

Why do we need so much drink and drugs?
Why do we have so much murder?
Will they ever solve all the problems?
Will they ever make this world better?

How many possessions do we need?
How much money must we procure?
Will we ever have all we would like?
Will we ever stop wanting more?

Why are our social attitudes wrong?
Why do we desire all we see?
Will our idols ever be virtuous?
Will we become all we should be?

Is?
   How?
      Will?
        Why?
          When?
            What have we become?

Harry Cameron (15)
Antrim Grammar School

Falling

Falling, falling,
Down through the sky
Falling, falling,
I think I'm very high,
Falling, falling,
Will I ever stop?
Falling, falling,
I guess not.

Falling, falling,
I'm in total despair
Falling, falling,
In this very cold air
Falling, falling,
Will anyone ever realise?
Falling, falling,
About those girls I despise.

Oh Lord, give me strength,
To forget about those girls
Who purposely hurt me.
I just wish it would stop
And to those girls
I would be forgot.

Lyndsey Hoe (13)
Antrim Grammar School

D-Day

I jump off the landing craft
Into the red murky water
The sand runs red with blood
I slice my leg on barbed wire
In the distance I see a man on fire
I turn to see someone shooting at me.

Andrew Cullen (13)
Antrim Grammar School

A Cry In War!

How many must cry in pain?
How many must suffer?
How long till the hard times are over?
How long till we can rejoice again?

Why did it all happen?
Why did it leave us startled?
Why is it hard to pick up where we left?
Why is it still not over?

Who hated us that much?
Who had something against us?
Who decided the innocent must suffer?
Who declared the war?

When will they leave us in peace?
When will they let us rebuild our lives?
When can everyone forgive them?
When can everyone smile?

What makes two countries fall out?
What makes others join in?
What is our country now?
What is a peaceful world?

Where is there a safe place to hide?
Where is there a safe place to walk?
Where is there a land not at war?
Where will we die?

Elspeth Woolsey (14)
Antrim Grammar School

Don't Be Afraid To Ask For Help . . .

He hears her screaming,
He hears the footsteps coming near,
He should have told someone,
But instead he hides in fear.

Tears rolling down his face,
But then as the giant walks in the room,
The giant booms,
'I need to put you in your place.'
The boy curls up in fear of him.

The door is flung open,
The giant walks in,
The boy asks for forgiveness,
But there is no reply and nothing from him,
The boy hides in fear,
Hiding his plain bruised face,
The only movement on it is his streaming tears,
That roll on down his face,
The giant swings his fist,
Leaving the boy's face far worse than ever before,
The pain in his face he has to embrace,
'You deserve it,' he says with a huge shout,
Then the giant storms out.

Why did it get this bad?
As the boy lies there lifeless,
The boy is tired and closes his eyes,
He can't be bothered anymore,
He is no longer fearless,

But then . . .

The faint sound of his sister's yelp
Why did it get to this state?
There are plenty of people who could help,
But for him, I'm very afraid, it's far too late.

Caitlin Weston (13)
Antrim Grammar School

The Glistening Sun And The Glittering Moon

It brightens up the summer's sky,
As we sing and play.
Pulling at our hearts of joy,
All throughout the day.

Silently it shines above,
As bluebirds sing their tune.
We listen to them carefully,
And welcome the new moon.

It glows in the darkened night,
And drifts across the black lagoon.
It fluently appears throughout the years,
Performing different moods.

Never seems to amaze us,
How beautiful they can be,
But without the joy and happiness,
They would never be.

Corinne Clark (16)
Antrim Grammar School

Waiting For Monday

She sits alone for hours on end,
For reasons of her own.
She waits and waits, but for what?
A happy woman she used to be,
So what has made her sad?
A man she knew but knows no more,
Has broken her inside.

They used to spend all day together,
But now he's nowhere to be seen.
He left her to fight for his country,
He left her for the army.
He told her he'd be back on Monday
And here she is, five years later,
Still waiting for Monday.

Michael Rutledge (14)
Antrim Grammar School

Holidays!

I'm going on my holiday
All the way to France,
I really am excited
I want to skip and prance.

Sunbathing by the hot tub,
All day until I burn,
Or maybe go on exciting slides
That make my stomach churn.

I'll go and play tennis -
It's a bit too warm for that,
But I really like the idea
Of swinging with my bat.

Perhaps I'll go on safari
Or maybe visit the park,
Or even the giant aquarium
Full of fish and sharks.

There's so much to do on my holidays
I just can't tell what to do first
But I am so full of excitement
So full I could literally burst!

Nicole Skilling (12)
Antrim Grammar School

Poetry!

P eople love reading poetry!
O nly when they are in the mood
E veryone enjoys reading poetry!
T rue . . . but not writing it!
R eading poetry is fun and enjoyable!
Y ehaa! I love poetry!

Rachel Kennedy (11)
Antrim Grammar School

The Country

I live in the country
The smell is beautiful - no smoke from cars or lorries
It is as quiet as a mouse, all you can hear
Is the soft moo of the cows,
And the gentle baa of the lambs skipping
In the field.

I love the country,
It is just so beautiful.
I live on a farm,
I have my own calves to feed
After I do my homework.
I have sheep and lambs
That I love to bits.

The country is the best
I would never leave it.
It is my home,
I enjoy every day when
I wake up and go
Out to work.

The country makes me
Feel older and more respected
So that is why I love
It so much.

Robert Smyth (12)
Antrim Grammar School

Autumn Is Coming

Autumn is clearly coming, I can feel it in my toes.
Nights are getting darker and the badgers are fattening up.
Squirrels collecting nuts and seeds for their winter stores.
Hedgehogs making homes to last the winter out.
Birds going south to get away from the cold,
And us buying clothes to keep us warm.

David Jones (12)
Antrim Grammar School

In The Sun

Hot, hot, holiday
Is such fun
Licking lollies
In the sun.

In the pool
Yippee
We run
It was such fun.
We lie in the sun,
Drop, drop, drop,
Oh no we run,
In out of the sun.

Rain, rain go to Spain
Never show your face again.
And guess what the rain
Went away
Yippee.

Brooke Getty (11)
Antrim Grammar School

My Little Cat

Some cats are tall,
Some cats are small,
But mine is very tiny.

Some coats are rough,
Some coats are soft,
But hers is very shiny.

When she starts to play,
She gets really naughty,
But she still is,
My lovely little cat.

Amit Jayaprakash (12)
Antrim Grammar School

School

School is the best,
That's what your parents say.
Voices filled with jest,
Best years of your life.
They claim.

But school is pointless,
With one single aim.
Destroy personalities
Make everyone the same.

Same uniform, same shoes,
Plain hair colour and tie.
Lots and lots of rules,
Do the teachers ever wonder why

When pupils rebel,
It's only to be put
In the silence of detention,
With all the other truants?

Continuous marking,
Improve, get better, be good,
Teachers always criticising,
Do you think they should?

Mouldy school dinners,
Pasta's never cooked.
Best years of our life?
I wish it wasn't pre-booked.

I want a time machine,
So I can skip school,
Then come back when I am leaving,
And decide if school is cool.

Lauren Milligan (13)
Antrim Grammar School

The Seasons

When it is spring,
Baby animals are born,
Little children on swings,
And farmers plant corn.

When it is summer,
It's very hot,
Don't wear fur,
Or you will rot.

When it is autumn,
Farmers harvest their crops,
'It's cold,' says Mum,
'Put on your warm tops.'

When it is winter,
The snow will fall,
Wear your coat made of fur,
It's hanging up in the hall.

Simon Wallace (12)
Antrim Grammar School

Noise

Woof! Woof!
Goes the dog next door!
Rustle! Rustle!
Goes the trees in the park!
Howl! Howl!
Goes the wind in the garden!
Sniffle! Sniffle!
Goes my little sister!
Chat! Chat!
Goes my mum on the phone!
Honk! Honk!
Goes the car outside!
Does a noise make a noise
If there is no one to hear it?

Lisha McNally (12)
Antrim Grammar School

Who, What, Where And Why?

Who, what, where and why?

'Who are you?
What are you?
Where are you?
Why are you there?'
'Leave me alone!'
'Why?'
'Because.'
'That's not a reason.'
'So?'
'No, why?'
'What are you doing?'
'Nothing.'
'You are!'
'I'm not.'
'Why are you lying?'
'I'm not!'
'Where are we?'
'Dunno.'
'Are we lost?'
'No!'
'Who is he?'
'I don't know.'
'Leave me alone!'
'Why?'

Courtney McCullough (11)
Antrim Grammar School

Hallowe'en

Hallowe'en is when the ghosts come
When the graveyards come alive
And all the skeletons come.
The evil presences scare people and they scream
The people run away but when the cockerel crows
All the evil returns to where it came from.

Adam Solari (12)
Antrim Grammar School

The Gymnast

The crowd cheers and claps,
As she steps out onto the floor,
She gracefully mounts the beam,
The crowd waits in anxious silence,
For her first move.

She turns a somersault,
And lands with such elegance and poise,
The crowd are stunned,
Next she leaps dramatically in the air,
And lands so softly on her feet.

Immediately she moves swiftly into a handstand,
She falls elegantly into a bridge,
Kicking over her legs,
She's back on her feet,
The crowd are intrigued.

For her next move she balances,
One leg high in the air, her arms outstretched,
Her final move is a backflip,
She gracefully dismounts.

Catherine Meers (11)
Antrim Grammar School

Race Cars

Race cars:
The smell of petrol and tyre smoke.
The arguments about who caused the crash.
Each driver is a nervous wreck before they go on the track.
The mechanic's worried, he might have to fix the car again,
The marshall waves the green flag,
The glory of winning's the best bit.

Ryan McCrory (11)
Antrim Grammar School

Hallowe'en

On this night out come horrors,
Horrors which scare people to their wit's end.
As the children are out in their costumes,
The creatures will fend, fend, fend.

Jumping from alleyways,
Breathing down your neck.
Waiting until you're all done,
So they can tear out your throat.

One day it will be you,
Dracula, a mummy and more,
Will be feasting on in a corner,
Whether you are rich or poor.

Each Hallowe'en the beasts come out,
But do have fun on this night.
Please don't be scared to go out,
But remember you must watch your back.

Niall McCulloch (12)
Antrim Grammar School

What I Like Most

What I like most
Is really good toast
Or my mum's roast,
But I'm not allowed to boast.

Umm, coffee -
Good with banoffee,
I also like toffee
And cappiccino when it's 'frothy'.

What I hate most
Is really bad toast
Or a burnt roast
And too hard toffee that smells like feet.

Liam McLoughlin (12)
Antrim Grammar School

Stop!

You're killing lives.
Look at me!
The truth never lies.
You will cut down this tree
Then another.
Where will you end
Your killing spree?
How many animals will
Suffer
Before you claim your fee?
Our world is
Dying
You keep denying
The truth.
We need to plant a future
Not destroy the present.
Cures are here to be found
Just look around.

Vanessa Brown (12)
Antrim Grammar School

Kingfisher

I see a dart of silver-blue
In the morning dew,
Off to catch his fish for today
In his graceful way.

Up in the bank I see his nest
Where he goes in the evening to rest
And where his family live.

I watch him diving swiftly down
In his majestic blue gown
He is quite a diver,
He's also a survivor.

Laura McBride (11)
Antrim Grammar School

The Bear

Once there was a bear with fuzzy hair
It was a bear without a care
It was as fat as the old lady's cat
Could you imagine a bear like that?

This bear was as clumsy as a clown
This bear was a darkish-brown
When this bear was in a bad mood
He just ate lots of food

This bear had its own bed
As well as his little Ted
When this bear found some meat
He got his fork and started to eat

When this bear woke up in its bed
He tried to get up but bumped his head
Then his honey started to decay
The bear exclaimed, 'This is not my day.'

Daniel Lewis (11)
Antrim Grammar School

The Unwanted Visitor

In the warmth of our house,
We heard the scratching of a mouse.
We looked for it here,
We looked for it there,
But we couldn't find it anywhere.
In the attic it made its home,
It even had my dad's old comb.
It ran about in my brother's room,
Before my dad whacked it with a broom.
During the day we thought it had gone,
But as we lay in our beds,
It partied all night long.

Daryl Mirza (11)
Antrim Grammar School

Myself

At school I am always quiet,
My classmates don't hear my voice a lot
They think I am shy.

My friends at home do hear my voice a lot
They know I never give up
And that I like to express my feelings
They know I am not shy.

My dance teacher believes in me
She always encourages me,
Helping and teaching me
She believes I am not shy

So when I am on stage
Performing and dancing
I am the one full of confidence
I am the one that stands out in the crowd.

Charlotte Allen (12)
Antrim Grammar School

Mystery Frost Man

On frosty nights in winter,
When it's cold and bitter.
He flies around the houses,
Looking for something to ice over with icy fingers.
His icy breath turns hands numb and cold,
He makes slippy paths glitter,
Stars twinkle and the night turns nippy,
Snowflakes fall from the sky.
His touch is as sharp as a butcher's knife,
Cutting through trees and bushes.
One touch of his finger,
Then ice appears spreading over everything.
He makes the leaves crackle and the grass crunch
This mystery man is
Jack Frost.

James McKee (11)
Antrim Grammar School

The Siege Of Tobruk

As we sat in our shallow trenches,
We tried to block out the sound of the twenty-five pounders,
As they exploded around us,
Failing to hit our artillery behind.

As the bell rang for the two hour ceasefire,
I raised my head trying to stretch my neck out,
I looked across at the Germans and saw them talking,
I wondered what was happening in the rest of the war,
Then the bell rang again for the end of the peace.

Word was spread that we were to raid an enemy pillbox,
I loaded my gun ready to go,
We ran across no-man's-land heading for the target,
The Germans opened fire, we chucked a grenade and ran.

Sometimes I wonder when this war will be over,
The blood, the killing and the fear,
When will this be over?

Alexander Arrell (12)
Antrim Grammar School

Worth Dying For?

The horrors of the Great World War
They thought it was worth dying for
With bodies falling all around,
And thuds as each one hits the ground
The shots are ringing through their heads
Another hit, another dead.
'Good shot,' they cry, another falls
The victim of their cannon balls
The taste of death swirls more and more -
What were they dying for?

Ellie Cameron (13)
Antrim Grammar School

The Jaguar

As it roars up the road,
My heart starts to beat.
When it comes to a halt,
The engine calmly becomes a sweet purr.

As I wait to see it,
The fire in my heart
Pumps with excitement.
I think to myself
What type is it?
How I long to know!

Then I see it
A British racing green V12 E-type Jag.
Its curves are perfect
Not a line out of place
Its seductive body says
'Look at me, a Jaguar.
A god among cars!'
It has a cream leather hood
With leather seats to match.

The purr then becomes a roar
As it speeds off
I think to myself, *That's from the 60s!*
What a wonderful age for cars!

Craig Lyness (12)
Antrim Grammar School

Myself

Me, me, me, me, me, me, me.
I love myself as you can see.
Oh how I love, me, me, me.
Me and myself share a real bond.
Of myself I'm incredibly fond!

David Friel (14)
Antrim Grammar School

Just A Lad

Everyone says, 'Hurry up,
You're running out of time.
You'll have to act with urgency,
You're already in year nine!
The decisions you make now,
Will affect all your later life.
Only rich, successful people,
Get a supermodel wife.
If you want to own a nice big house,
And drive a flashy car,
Make sure each and every homework,
Comes back with an 'A Star'.'
But I cannot see the point of it,
It's sure to end in tears.
To sacrifice my childhood,
And wish away the years.
I promise to work hard at school,
And respect my mum and dad.
But at holidays and weekends,
I just like being a lad!

Jimmy Elliott (12)
Antrim Grammar School

Myself

Not a perfect creation,
Sometimes rude,
Sometimes dishonest,
But unique.

An amazing creation,
Superior to all animals,
The most developed,
The most destructive.

James Patterson (14)
Antrim Grammar School

Myself

I am, who I am
But in myself I feel broken
Hurt and mocked I cry
I have lost all sense of confidence.

When I open my eyes
They fill with tears
This has happened
For many, many years.

I am, who I am
But in myself I feel broken
I am, who I am
But in myself, myself
I feel broken.

Look what you've done
You've wrecked my life
You've made me sad.

I'm not, I'm not
I'm not, myself.

Caroline Bingham (12)
Antrim Grammar School

Guide Me

Could you please guide me?
I cannot see.
I've never seen the stars
Or the moon's magical powers.
I've never seen the trees
And those beautiful autumn leaves.
I've never seen the snow
And the colours of things I do not know.
I've never seen you
Or the sky ever so blue
So I ask you please guide me . . .
I cannot see.

Alison Lawther (12)
Antrim Grammar School

A Poem

I was asked to do a poem
And I'm sitting here in thought
I'm trying to think back
On all the things I've been taught.

I could write about a lazy cat
Or an actor or a queen
However, I can think of nothing
It's awful, I could scream . . .

I would love to write a lovely poem
That I could be proud of, you see.
A long one, a rhyming one
Or one about what I would like to be.

However, I will never know
As I sit here at my desk
And I know I have to do my best
To beat the rest!

Leah Smyth (13)
Antrim Grammar School

The Machine Gun

All the people I shot dead,
The ground's become a mighty bed.
No one wakes at my scream,
I surely must be in a dream.
Then the gas comes tumbling down,
But still I shoot while they drown.
Blood comes dribbling down my side,
My operator has just died.
Many more will come and go,
Until I send my final blow.

Rachel Cadden (13)
Antrim Grammar School

Sophie's So Spoilt!

Sophie and I fell out the other day
She wants everything to go her way
We went to the teacher Ms Perry
She wasn't very caring
And told us to sort it out ourselves.

When that didn't work we went to Mr McCann
He always has a plan,
He said, 'The next time that we argue
'He' will come to haunt you!'

The question we ask is, 'Who is 'he'?'
He says that we will see
We've now decided not to argue,
Or else 'he' will come to haunt me!

Megan Heaney (12)
Antrim Grammar School

Street Cars

Cars are great,
Especially fancy souped ones,
My favourite, the Evo VIII
Or is it the Lamborghini Diablo?

Well, I guess I couldn't really pick,
Most of them are really slick.
They're even better with NOS,
Yeah, that makes them the boss.

What a thrill when you're racing,
To you 70mph is like you're pacing.
Kick in the NOS before the bridge and you're flying,
You only have to worry about crashing and dying!

Conor Ferry (12)
Antrim Grammar School

A Memory

In this poem I'd like to describe
Things I remember, things on my mind,
A memory is a treasured thought
A feeling like this could never be bought.

I remember the time I cried -
Do you remember the time a loved one died?
A memory is a treasured thought
A feeling like this could never be bought.

Although a memory I have mentioned
Not all memories have bad intention,
A memory is a treasured thought
A feeling like this could never be bought.

I remember in hockey, the first time I scored
And the time you called round when I felt sick and was bored,
A memory is a treasured thought
A feeling like this could never be bought.

Whenever I go to sleep at night
I think of things from the past like the party or the fight,
A memory is a treasured thought
A feeling like this could never be bought.

In this poem I have described
Things I remember, things on my mind,
A memory is a treasured thought
A feeling like this can never be bought.

Grace Shannon (13)
Antrim Grammar School

Football

Football, oh football, it makes you grow tall.
It's better than being stuck, oh so small.
Football, oh football, it's great for the heart
It's also good for making you smart.
Football, oh football, I love you so much
You're played all the time by the very skilled Dutch.
Football, oh football, you're great, you are fun,
At last Saturday's match my brilliant team won!
Football, oh football, and winning the cup,
As a reward my parents gave me a pup.
Football, oh football, it makes you grow strong
Then you're able to hit the ball long.
Football, oh football, I hit the bar
But then again I aimed from afar.
Football, oh football, we just scored a goal
A lovely header from my friend Noel.
Football, oh football, the whistle has blown
If you've just lost then go crying off home.

James Montgomery (11)
Antrim Grammar School

War

The guns were fired
The soldiers tired
The war seemed never to end.
The soldiers dying
Their families crying
The human race
Won't be safe.
When will mankind learn
To turn from war
And find reason
And peace?

Alistair Steele (13)
Antrim Grammar School

A Weekend At Army Cadet Camp

A weekend at army cadet camp . . .
The potatoes were all mushy
And the beds were cold and hard
The rifles were fantastic but they were very tall
The PE court was a hangar in it was the games
But when it was all over I wanted home again
Madam called me a giant though I was very small . . .
At home again I went to bed
I had to rest my weary head.

Scott McDowell (12)
Antrim Grammar School

The Trail Of Death

As he's trailed away by Death,
Dirty, smelly and such a mess,
He's frightened and scared and all alone,
As he's trailed over the dead that moan,
As they do nothing he sits and cries,
He hopes his family aren't told any lies,
As all, he knows what lies in store,
He only wishes he had time before.

Nicola Campbell (13)
Antrim Grammar School

Rock

I love to play my electric guitar,
I turn it full blast in the car,
When I'm older my dream is to be,
A rock star like Jon Bon Jovi.

I like to listen to the Rolling Stones,
I've got their tunes on my phones,
I would like to be in a band,
And do concerts in every land.

Supreet Jayaprakash (13)
Antrim Grammar School

Wintertime

I got up in the morning, looked out of the window
The snow was falling very heavily
The snowflakes looked so crisp and clean
I very quickly put on my warm clothes.

I ran outside
Every step I took all I could hear was
Crunch, crunch, crunch,
And little 'Robbie Robin' singing in the background.

All my friends came outside
We all sprinted down to the lake
It was all frozen
It reminded me of an ice lolly.

As I looked around the snow was so beautiful
And white and crisp and clean
It seemed to be sprinkled over everything I'd seen
But it reminded me of a big beautiful Christmas cake.

Jessica Johnston (11)
Antrim Grammar School

Death

Crack!
The sound echoes down the alley.
I fall to my knees as my strength flies from me.
My shooter flees from the alley in fear that he may be caught.
The blood stains my shirt like a dark red flower.
My head hits the ground and blood spills from my mouth.
Then I hear the sound of sirens.
I hang on, hoping that I still might be saved.
But the sirens fade into the distance.
Knowing all is lost, I give in to the ever increasing darkness.
I see my life flashing before my eyes.

Then there is no pain, but peace . . .

Thomas Finn (13)
Antrim Grammar School

My Day

Today I went to school to learn
I learnt about moss and fern
I did boring maths, for what felt like all day
I was so happy when we got out to play.

It's the big test,
I'll try my best,
I did lots of work
To find no perk.

I watched TV for a while,
I sorted out my washing pile.
And now I am writing this out
Yet on my face I still wear a pout.

Now the day has come to an end
And my sister is driving me round the bend.

Nicola McKee (13)
Antrim Grammar School

Flower In The Flowerpot

Flower in the flowerpot growing to its knees,
Flower in the flowerpot blowing in the breeze,
Flower in the flowerpot looking very small,
Flower in the flowerpot growing up tall,
Flower in the flowerpot flourishing in the sun,
Flower in the flowerpot innocent as a nun,
Flower in the flowerpot swinging in the air,
Flower in the flowerpot not a bit bore,
Flower in the flowerpot a beautiful sight,
Flower in the flowerpot out in the night,
Flower in the flowerpot counting some sheep,
Flower in the flowerpot has gone to sleep.

Gavin Ward (11)
Antrim Grammar School

Us Girls

We're supposed to love pink
And be so innocent
But some girls break the mould
Really the truth is;
Some girls talk about each other
Some girls leave others out
Some girls think they're the best
Some girls are just judgmental
But the message I leave you,
Is, never change yourself
Stay the way you are
No matter what some girls think,
Say or do,
Remember you're a star,
Block your ears and don't listen
Us girls can be so cruel.

Emily Adams (13)
Antrim Grammar School

Chips

Chips are tasty,
Chips are nice,
Chips taste of chips
Which tastes tasty and nice.

Chips are crunch,
Chips are crisp,
Chips taste of chips
Which are crunch and crisp.

Chips taste heavenly,
Chips taste creamy,
Chips taste of chips
Which are heavenly and creamy.

Chips are yummy!

Becky Seawright (11)
Antrim Grammar School

My Family

I have a little sister
Whose name is Sammy-Joe
She has a huge fat blister
On her biggest toe.

I have a bigger brother
His name is Sammy-Sam
He lives on a diet
Of slippy, sloppy spam.

My daddy is an actor
One day he went to try
To get into the X-Factor
They told him, 'Thank you and bye.'

My mother is a classical singer
She loves to sing and prance
But when I turn rock music on
She always wets her pants!

I've got a little doggy
He's really very cute
But the chap who sold him to us
He only had one foot.

Alice Irvine (11)
Antrim Grammar School

Poems

If I were to think all day
I would have a lot to say
That is what a poem is about
If I were to write ten lines
It would be fine
That is what a poem is about
Well can't write ten lines
I don't want to think all day
So this is all I'm going to say

Naomi Camlin (12)
Antrim Grammar School

4-4-2

The guy in goal,
Must be as tall as a pole,
With hands as safe as houses.

The defending four,
Should be as wide as a door,
And can't be big girls' blouses.

The men in the middle,
Have to be as fit as a fiddle,
And cover the pitch as a whole.

And while the two who are striking,
May be as quick as lightning
There's no substitute for a goal.

Lewis Brammeld (11)
Antrim Grammar School

My Magic Snowman

When I went to bed last night,
I had the most amazing fright,
When I looked out of my window,
The sky just began to snow.

In the morning I woke up,
I was so excited, I jumped up,
The snow was lying on the ground,
Not making a single sound.

So last night I built a snowman,
Then I went to bed,
When I woke up in the morning,
My poor snowman was *dead!*

Naomi Jones (11)
Antrim Grammar School

Fish

Fish in the sea,
Big and small,
Fat and thin,
Short and tall.
Swim round and round
No care in the world.
Until . . .

Swimming fast through the water
Towards the carefree fish,
Sharp teeth, dark body,
Quietly gliding to its snack,
Getting closer, then . . . *munch!*
What a tasty lunch.

Carrie McClenaghan (13)
Antrim Grammar School

My Family

This bit is about my mum,
Who thinks she has a big bum,
My mum is the one who pays the bills,
And my cakes and sweets at the tills.

This section is about my dad,
Who can go slightly mad.
When he is terribly drunk,
His breath smells like a skunk.

The final bit is about my brother,
Who always cuddles up to my mother,
I think he came from the wild,
Because he is a mad child.

Aden Howe (11)
Antrim Grammar School

My School

Antrim Grammar is a good school
Some of the subjects are really cool.
My favourite subject is PE
We play games such as hockey.
Before we play hockey we have to run
Around the pitch
Before we can have fun.

Another subject I learn is history
We have learnt about
William, Duke of Normandy
Who won a famous battle
But also stole some Englishmen's castle.

During my stay I hope to have fun
I wish the same for everyone!

Rebecca Hoban (12)
Antrim Grammar School

Why War?

Devastation and destruction,
Death is all around.

Bomb craters, shattered trees,
Bodies on the ground.

We fight to save our brothers,
To give them back their land.

We fight to give them freedom,
And release from German hands.

But scrambling through the muddy hollows,
As we struggle to be free.

The evil German searchlights,
Mean this may not be.

Amanda Monteith (13)
Antrim Grammar School

Hallowe'en Happenings

In the pitch-black sky the moon shines bright,
Strange things happen on Hallowe'en night.
Noises in the distance are scary and eerie,
The night is cold and dark and dreary.

Listen to the clatters and rattles of a skeleton's bones.
Evil barks and weird groans.
Pumpkins in the dark are glimmering and gleaming,
Hear the sound of children screaming.

Children are out yelling, 'Trick or treat!'
Collecting lots of yummy sweets.
Dressing up in costumes and pointy hats,
See the spiders, rats and bats.

Witches making brew in their magic pots,
Its gurgles, gargles, splish and splosh.
With ghouls; and ghosts lurking near
Hallowe'en is a scary time of year!

Elizabeth Cartwright (12)
Antrim Grammar School

A Poem On Antrim Grammar School

Antrim Grammar is a really good school,
We do loads of subjects - some are cool
Maths, English and also RE
History, music and geography
Some I like and some I don't
Things you want to do and things you won't.
We do technology, games and PE
In games, Year 8 do rugby.
There are some after school activities
They start when school ends at 10 past 3
The library has lots of books and is big
From 'Lord of the Rings' to 'Percy the Pig'
We have to be in school by 8.45
And just hope that at 10 past 3 we will be alive!

Gareth Gould (11)
Antrim Grammar School

Hallowe'en Night

The darkness of the night
Not a light in sight,
Not a person to be seen
But wait, here is something -
What could it possibly have been?

When I turned down Elm Street
There was no one there, just a hare
In the middle of the square.

I turned to look towards the graveyard
There were flashing lights all around,
Three things stood guarding the gate,
But wait, they were not alive
They were dead!

The night came to an end,
Or did it?
That is the question,
Do you have an answer?

Ryan Richardson (11)
Antrim Grammar School

My Favourite Car (The Kröienburg)

It does 240 mph (miles per hour)
And 15 mpg (miles per gallon)
It's a four seater
What a heart beater
And it's got looks to kill.

It's the fastest street loyal car in the world
No one comes near it
You are lucky to hear it
When it's going down the roads of Sweden
There's only one problem with my dream car
There are only seven made.

Karl Morris (12)
Antrim Grammar School

Friends!

A friend to me is a person
You can trust,
They understand you and
Everything you do.
They accept you for nothing
Less than you want them to.
They stick up for you when
Times get rough,
And know how to deal with you
When you are in a huff.
To me a friend is someone
You can turn to
When you are feeling down
They can guarantee to wipe
Away your frown.
As many people would say,
'Friends are the family we choose for ourselves.'

Zara Morrow (11)
Antrim Grammar School

War

War is a terrible brutal thing,
The guns start to fire and your ears start to ring,
Your friends are gunned down -
They fall to the ground
And you feel all alone in the world.
You dream of home
You miss your mum -
But the war keeps going on.
Soon I will be gone
And I will be gunned down,
I will fall to the ground
And the shells won't blast
Because I'll be at peace, at last.

Ashley Knapper (13)
Antrim Grammar School

Season Feeling

The grass is growing,
The blue sky is showing.
These both happen in spring.

The warmth of the sun,
The smell of lavender.
Spring is all around us.

No snow in sight,
The sun shines bright.
The winter is long gone.

The tulips shoot up,
The birds swoop down.
These are the symptoms of spring.

Lambs in the field,
Calves lie on hay.
Oh, what a lovely spring day.

The sweet sound of birds,
And the white clouds in the sky.
This is a beautiful spring.

Rachel Walker (12)
Antrim Grammar School

Animals

A nimals are cool
N asty
I ndependent
M an's best friend
A mazing
L oud, but they do
S leep.

James Woolsey (11)
Antrim Grammar School

God!

A life without God,
Is a life unlived!
A life with God,
Is a life to enjoy!

Trust in him always,
Because if you don't,
You might end up,
As sad,
As sad as sad can be!

Praise and worship,
Is something he needs,
Because if you don't praise him,
He might feel let down!

So don't forget him,
Or let him down,
But most of all,
Don't forget him,
Even in a dream!

Ryan Peacock (11)
Antrim Grammar School

My Sister

My sister is my best pal
She is such a brilliant gal,
My sister is such a laugh
She can also be very daft,
My sister is so loving and caring,
She can also be very daring,
If I'm ever in need, I would give her a call
Because I love my sister most of all.

Robyn Foster (12)
Antrim Grammar School

I'm Different

I'm different in my own special way,
I live my own life, make my own day.
I don't need to be a girl - popular and pretty,
I don't need to be sweet or cute like a kitty.
I'll laugh when I want, cry when I feel,
I'm my own person, grounded and real.

I know you all look and stare,
Or act like you don't know I'm there.
You raise eyes at where my belly shows,
Or smirk at the piercing in my nose.
I'll look how I like, dress how I feel,
I'm seen as my own person, grounded and real.

I see you all look and laugh at my friends,
But at least my mates don't care about trends.
My mates don't ditch me when I say the wrong thing,
My friends keep their promises when they say they'll ring.
I'll like who I want and find friends where I choose,
I'm my own person, and this I'll never lose.

Helen Peden (12)
Antrim Grammar School

Cherries

Cherries, cherries, delicious little cherries,
They are the best out of all the berries,
But inside these cherries there are stones,
Big enough to rattle your bones,
Inside again there is the taste,
Too delicious to let them go to waste,
When it comes to the very best berry,
I have to say it is the cherry.

Alannah Stirling (11)
Antrim Grammar School

The Titanic

The Titanic was the greatest ship,
These are the words from everyone's lips.
It sailed across the Atlantic sea,
Not knowing its true destiny.
The ship was heaven, this unsinkable boat,
Never capsize, just stay afloat.
The Titanic came, the iceberg it hit,
While people socialise, as they sit.
The ice from the iceberg fell onto the ship,
For people to fall and for people to slip.

The iceberg left a hole in the boat,
The ship of dreams did not stay afloat.
As the ship sank into deep waters,
Lifeboats were filled with women and their daughters.
Little boys were allowed on as well,
As the warning bell went off - that deafening bell.
It was as if their lives had ended,
Lives which had just begun, could not be mended.
As Titanic was swallowed into the blue,
It carried away a life or two.
The Titanic was the unsinkable boat,
Until that day, it did not float.

James Hyde (12)
Antrim Grammar School

Brothers In War D-Day!

They ran onto the beach expecting death,
But nevertheless they keep fighting,
They see their friends slaughtered beside them,
Weary that they may suffer the same fate,
They hide, take cover and think about war,
They aim with their rifles and take a shot,
But their rifle locks,
They served their time in Hell!

Patrick Lecky (12)
Antrim Grammar School

A Winglebingle

I once met a winglebingleologist,
Who had a very bony wrist,
From writing these things on a list.

A winglebingle lives on a shingle,
A winglebingle is never single,
A winglebingle likes to mingle,
A winglebingle makes you tingle.

It is red, yellow, green and orange,
And not to forget the colour borange,
Which is a mixture of blue and orange.

A winglebingle is very friendly,
And when it is happy, it hums like a Bentley.

To tell you very gently,
I study winglebingles because they are friendly,
And I always have dreamt of getting a Bentley.

Hayley Carole Donaldson (12)
Antrim Grammar School

The Ghost

The ghost, it sat at the back of the classroom,
No one knew it was there.
The ghost, it sat at the back of the classroom,
It used to sit and stare.

The ghost, it sat at the back of the classroom,
It sat there every week.
The ghost, it sat at the back of the classroom,
It's said to look like a geek.

The ghost, it sat at the back of the classroom,
It was called William O'Haire
The ghost, it sat at the back of the classroom,
Now it is not there.

Rebecca Steele (11)
Antrim Grammar School

The Months

January is the first
People eating, fit to burst.

February is the second,
Water's freezing, people reckon.

March is full of melting ice,
Spring is coming, that will be nice.

Sun starts in April,
Buds appear on the maples.

The month of May is full of surprises,
The school fair's coming, I can win prizes.

June is when the days grow,
People remove their shoes and show their toes.

July is when the weather's hot,
Everyone wears big coats - not!

August is full of laughter and mirth,
Many people learn to surf.

September is the end of summer,
Most people become glummer.

October ends with Hallowe'en,
Mum dressed up as a dead old queen.

November is a rainy month,
The sun did shine but only once.

Christmas is December joy
Now I'll go and play with my new toy.

Jake Smith (11)
Antrim Grammar School

Midnight Scare!

It's late at night,
I hear a noise,
Whatever could it be?
It's getting louder and more clearer,
I think it's after me.

It's coming from my closet,
Where dark things like to creep.
I try to ignore it,
But I still can't get to sleep.

I know it wants out,
Why else would it cry?
It's going to get out,
I'm going to die.

The door swings open,
I hear a loud bang.
Something lands on my bed,
It's my little cat, Fang.

Kerri Moore (11)
Antrim Grammar School

Fire

Fire! Fire! Burning bright,
In the forest in the night.

Fire! Fire! Gleaming yellow
The colour looking oh, so mellow.

Fire! Fire! Crackles rich,
Makes me become bewitched.

Fire! Fire! Cosy and warm
Just like a heated dorm.

Rebecca Docherty (12)
Antrim Grammar School

The Seasons

We'll start with winter
In darkness, no light
Completely concealed
Nothing in sight.

Then things will brighten
We'll come into spring
Beauty all around
It will make you sing.

We're now in summer
It's getting ever so warm
Bees collecting honey
All in a swarm.

As we come into autumn
The leaves will come down
It's time to play,
Brown and orange all around.

Now we're in winter
Our cycle starts again
This wonderful phenomenon
That is certainly not plain!

Natalie Parke (11)
Antrim Grammar School

My Mum

My mum works hard for me,
Cares for me,
And loves me.
Sometimes I just don't realise
How much she does for me,
As well as my two older brothers.
So I just want you to think about
All the things your mum does for you,
After you read this poem.

Judith Patterson (11)
Antrim Grammar School

My Horse Poem

As I gazed out of my window to the fields below,
I see a lonely horse
Grazing in the meadow.

I stroke the chestnut head,
I comb its long brown hair.
Then I unlock the latch,
And the energetic horse runs wild and free,
It doesn't care!

The horse gallops in the field,
Racing with the wind.
I hear the thunder of hooves,
And I see its hair shining and blowing with the wind.

Its brilliant bright auburn eyes follow me,
Around the meadow.
I get on its back and it canters in the daylight,
And as we pass all the trees, animals and hedges,
I see my reflection in the blue gleaming lake.

I dream about horses every night
I think about horses during the day
Particularly this one,
Always.

I picture us together
Beside the gleaming lake.
No matter what the weather,
That's all that I could take!

Victoria Howarth (12)
Antrim Grammar School

Hallowe'en

A dark spooky night,
The sun's gone out of sight.
The moon has come out,
Suddenly there's an eerie shout.
There's something out there in the dark,
There's a horrible shriek and an evil bark.
Out come some white shapes, 1, 2, 3,
Coming across the lawn, coming near to me.
'Trick or treat,' they evilly cry.
Some more creatures walk by.
The doorbell rings all through the night,
They all walk around with a pumpkin light.
My mum gives out lots of treats,
Toffee apples and plenty of sweets.
Hallowe'en looks like plenty of fun,
I don't think I need to hide or run.

Anna Gardiner (11)
Antrim Grammar School

Sally-Ann

Sally-Ann walking down the street
She smiles at everyone she meets.
If you fall she'll help you up,
People always stop and stare,
At this little girl so full of care.

Her smile is syrupy sweet,
She's the nicest girl you could ever meet.
Sometimes older kids stop and jeer,
But she never seems to hear.

Sally-Ann's as good as gold,
Spitting, screaming, shouting, never!
We hoped she'd stay here forever,
But a big van came down the road one day,
And Sally-Ann moved away.

Lauren Patton (12)
Antrim Grammar School

Hallowe'en

Now once again it's that time of the year
When the towns and the streets are filled with fear.
It's only once a year on an October night,
When your whole body is overcome with fright.

Hallowe'en is the time when the kids trick or treat,
And at the end of the night their bags are filled with sweets,
It is at this time the pumpkins come out
And it is at this time the spirits scream and shout.

Hallowe'en is the time when the fireworks are lit
And lots of people go to parties in their Hallowe'en outfits.
Hallowe'en is the time when you decorate your hall
It's the time of the year when everyone has a ball.

Hallowe'en is the time when everyone is scared.

Boo!

Gareth Holden (12)
Antrim Grammar School

What Is Magic?

Magic is the sunshine that pours through the trees,
Magic is the dance in the cool autumn breeze.

Magic is the sparkle in a mischievous child's eye,
Magic is when the eagle soars through the sky.

Magic is the deep blue depths of the sea,
That is what magic is to me,

Some people say magic is a man with a tall top hat,
But there are many things more magical than that.

Laura Dempster (12)
Antrim Grammar School

Dogs

Dogs are playful,
They are fun to be with.
Dogs are my favourite animal,
They come in lots of different colours and sizes.
I have a dog; her name is Tess
She is thirteen (very old for a dog).
She is a cross between a German shepherd and a Border collie.
My dog is really smart,
Even though she is old she still plays ball with me.
You would think she would hate cats
But she doesn't hate them,
She licks them, protects them and plays with them.
Dogs are playful.
They are fun to be with.
Dogs
The best animal in the world.

Hannah Fletcher (11)
Antrim Grammar School

Rugby

Brian O'Driscoll, what a guy,
He knows what's happening all the time.
The scrum-half Peter Stringer,
Is as nifty as a dodgy springer
When the prop, big John Hayes,
Runs with people, they go with a daze.

I play rugby at Randalstown.
In our last match we won 3-2 from 2-0 down.
Our coach Neil is the best coach we've had,
He's better than our last coach, he was really bad!
Mark and Martin, Adam and me,
All part of the Randalstown team.

Paul Duncan (11)
Antrim Grammar School

The Dragon

I am a warrior from a land far away.
My dream is to become a legend in this land
So I'm going to the king to see what he will say,
About me going to a place with beaches full of sand.
For on that island, there's a dragon I will slay,
The king says, 'Yes,' but I just might
Need a weapon to win this fight.
I buy a good sword from my local blacksmith,
However, he thought that dragons were a myth.
But I know better than that.
I'm off to the island with dragons, caves and bats.
Now I am there, the time has come
For me to fight this fire-breathing dragon.
I go into a cave, which is his lair.
I deal the first hit, from behind.
It must have hit hard, for he whipped around,
After one breath of fire, I am toast,
I think I am his Sunday roast.
He grabs me with his big, long tail,
In a last thought I begin to wail.
He drops me in his mouth
And I am no more.
My bones now lie on the cave floor.

Chael McLean (13)
Antrim Grammar School

Cheetah

We watch in awe
As he whizzes by,
His spots turn to lightning streaks
As he hunts down the thunderous wildebeest.

With a jump and a leap
He takes one down
His mission complete,
And we can only watch in awe.

Malin Murphy (12)
Antrim Grammar School

Autumn Colours

One late autumn evening
In a farmhouse built strong
The old farmer lay sleeping
In front of the warm, roaring fire.

Soon, morning time comes,
And the sun rises up above the mountains.
The calves in the fields
All frisk in the leaves,
Coloured red, yellow, orange and green.

As the farmer waves up he has a pleasant surprise,
The sun is shining through his window.
Now as he walks through his fields he finds
A hedgehog rolling in the crisp autumn leaves.
The farmer stands still for a moment
Looking at the autumn colours.

Catherine Gawn (11)
Antrim Grammar School

Hallowe'en Night

Hallowe'en is a scary night
When all the pumpkins are alight,
When children come out to trick or treat
And fill their bags with lovely sweets,
Glittery fireworks fly into the night,
And the sparklers are set alight.
The ghosts and ghouls are out to scare you,
So be careful I will beware you.
When in bed,
Tucked up tight,
Remember to be careful on
Hallowe'en night.

Katherine Gould (11)
Antrim Grammar School

Rugby

Rugby is a fun game
Passing the ball, that's the aim,
Tackle tough, ball alive,
That's when Antrim Grammar thrive.

Rugby is a tough game
The referee gets the blame.
Rucking, driving, sportsmanship
Let's all be in the Hornets' Ship.

Andrew Patterson (12)
Antrim Grammar School

Rugby

Winning, winning, that's the aim
That's the challenge in every game,
Running hard and scoring tries
'No, please don't,' the other team cries.

Passing, passing, needs a straight line -
To hear teammates call, 'The ball is mine,'
Celebrations at the end,
As we drive our own coach round the bend.

Timothy Woolsey (12)
Antrim Grammar School

Why?

Why do children go to school?
Why do our parents never act cool?
Why do girls always talk about each other?
Why do our siblings get us into bother?
Why do our parents embarrass us in front of boys?
Why do teachers always complain about noise?
There are many things we don't understand . . .
Why?

Debbie Quigley (12)
Antrim Grammar School

Paths Of Glory

(Based on the painting 'Paths of Glory' by Christopher Nevinson)

We joined the army, my friend and I,
Our hopes for glory were sky-high.
We were to be 'famous', 'well paid' and 'well fed',
At least, that's what the posters said.

In reality, war is actually a fight to survive,
At least my friend and I are still alive.
War's a competition to get the biggest gun,
They think that killing people is supposed to be fun.

We wonder, with all our guns, do the Germans really fear us?
Suddenly a German shell explodes near us.
My friend falls to the ground and so do I,
Now, on the 'Paths of Glory', we are both going to die.

Emma McFadden (14)
Antrim Grammar School

Time

You cannot smell, taste or feel time,
And it is not seen or heard,
But the idea that time does not exist,
Well, that is just absurd.

They say that if you are having fun,
Then the time will fly,
But a second lasts a second and an hour lasts an hour,
That you cannot deny.

Time is a weird and wonderful thing,
It is enough to drive you insane,
The time that you have spent reading this poem,
You will never get back again.

Mark Lewis (13)
Antrim Grammar School

Friends

Everyone needs a friend or two,
To catch them when they fall
To help them up when they're down
Anything at all.

I felt broken in half
Slit down the middle
Torn into a thousand pieces.

My best friend had gone
She was never coming back
Instead it was this completely different girl.

She is loud, flirty
And even quite cheeky
A completely different attitude.

For a while I felt lost
Stranded, a loner,
I had collapsed on a bed of nails.

But now I have been lifted
Up higher than ever
By a brand new set of friends.

Now a year has passed by
I'm always on high
With true friends by my side.

My life's never been better
I've had a major sugar overload
All with true friends by my side.

Everyone needs a friend or two
To catch them when they fall
To help them up when they're down
Anything at all.

Amy Adams (12)
Antrim Grammar School

Homeless

In the corner hurt and bare
Sits that sad little girl
No one loves her
No one cares
About that sad little girl.

In the alley, dirty and poor
Sits the lonely little boy
No one loves him
No one cares
About that little boy.

Someone help them before it's too late
And save them from their terrible fate.

Emma Osborne (12)
Antrim Grammar School

A Winter's Night

Snow falling swiftly,
The whitest of the white,
Moonlight making it sparkle,
On this winter's night.
Smoke rising from chimneys,
In front of the glistening stars.
The sky is a deep blue,
Above the sleeping flowers.
The street lights are humming,
By the roadsides on their own.
The wind is whistling
And making a low-pitched moan.

James Fulton (11)
Antrim Grammar School

The Enzo

Smooth to the touch,
Pleasing to the eye,
As it zooms on by.
Designed to perfection,
Built with such precision,
Perfect for my collection.
The Ferrari Enzo,
My favourite car,
It's such a star.
With a max speed of 230 mph
And equipped with a V12 engine,
Streamlined to perfection,
Every little section,
Perfect for my collection.

Jack Parte (12)
Antrim Grammar School

Spirit Of The Tiger

Roar! echoed from his cage
Young 'uns are scared from his rage
I can understand why . . .
He was captured from an open sky
His freedom taken, now it's gone
Like in chess, he is just a pawn.

Being kept in captivity
Does not have much activity.
I would definitely assume
He would have to suffer in gloom.
Now the tiger is nearly dead
There is nothing more to be said.

Ben Lewis (12)
Antrim Grammar School

Jimmy Jumpy

There once was a white monkey
His name was Jimmy Jumpy
He jumped all day
And he jumped all night
Until he learned the power of flight
Now he flies all day
And he flies all night
But his future does not look bright
For when he flew
He got attacked with glue
So his fur now looks blue
He is called Jimmy the flying blue monkey
Tourists say he's funky
But when he dies
He will not fly
And will still be called Jimmy Jumpy.

Liam Hind (13)
Antrim Grammar School

A Doggy

If you have a doggy,
Who likes to swim,
Take him to the river
And throw him in.

But, you better watch
He doesn't drown
Because then you'll
Have to go back to the pound!

David Brown (12)
Antrim Grammar School

What Is War All About?

Marching to their destination,
Hearts full of courage for their nation,
But do they know about the fight?
The fight they'll fight with all their might.

Getting all their weapons prepared,
Marching bravely as if they're not scared,
Oblivious to the bombs being hurled,
Marching on without a care in the world.

In the trenches they will go,
Soon they will be covered in dirt from head to toe.
All the carnage, all the destruction,
Families at home saying, 'We love you so much, Son.'

Men side by side of all ages,
Encouraged to fight and be courageous,
Defending their families against the mayhem,
So maybe some day they can be back with them.

All the mothers think of their brave sons,
But do they really want them fighting with guns,
They really don't have a clue,
Of the terror their sons are going through.

Men fighting bravely,
Friends dying gravely,
What is war all about?
Why are men fighting for all they're worth?

Martha Watson (14)
Ballyclare High School

Separation

Their wives and daughters say goodbye
For king and country they will die
No more family, no more love
In the trench death came from above.

Sam Burnison (15)
Ballyclare High School

Tanya

There once was a dog of strength, bravery and playfulness . . .

She had a cold wet nose, a chocolate-brown fluffy coat and a long
waggy tail.

When I was born she was nearly a year old,
And was excited about my arrival.
Slowly as I grew, this fluffy wonder taught
Me the aspects of life and guarded my every move.

She was a guardian angel and a best friend
So much more than just a dog.
There was not a single bad hair on her body.
She was my world and that world fell apart,
When I heard she had cancer in her leg bone.
I thought I would lose my baby . . .
Luckily there was a way to save her - amputate her leg.

In March, Tanya became one leg less but
It didn't affect her - she was a fighter.
She was still my wonderful, friendly guardian angel even with only three
legs!

She walked this world for only five more months before
The dreaded cancer struck again in her lungs and took my love away.
With a lick to the hand and a quiet whimper,
She left our world after fifteen years of devoted loyalty
And never-ending friendship.

I know she is still watching over me,
My darling Tanya, and is waiting for me at the Rainbow Bridge.
Her youth restored and playing happily,
With her doggie friends until I meet her there.
Then we will cross the Rainbow Bridge to
Our final resting place, together again forever.

Dawn Comins (14)
Ballyclare High School

The Moon Shines Bright

When the moon shines bright
And the stars, they follow.
Into the woods we go
Then down to the lake
Through a gap in the trees
You can see the moon shine bright
Onto the water to stare at the stars
Far away from our world of cars
Pause and look at the stars and the moon
Let them soothe you to sleep
And you will be asleep soon
When the moon shines bright
Even when the wind howls
And it is covered by a cloud
The moon will always shine bright.

Ryan Cooke (14)
Ballyclare High School

What's The Point?

The roar of the rifle fire
The lion that never tires
Hunting its prey day and night
For a belief that's neither wrong, nor right.

Once it's caught death, it is fast
But hunger returns it never lasts
Destruction, famine, the end of a race
But the powers to be make it gather pace.

No one wins, no one loses
The common man, it's death that chooses
Women and children their loves anoint
War, war, war, what's the point?

Stuart Greer (14)
Ballyclare High School

Northern Ireland Vs England

Northern Ireland against England was the match
England made a quick attack
Everyone in the stadium was excited
Ireland cleared and we were delighted.

Northern Ireland were on the back hand for most of the match
It was a great half and a good laugh,
They got their occasional sight at goal
But it was an excellent half for Ashley Cole.

The fans were cheering
As both teams were fearing
The commentators could not choose
Which team was going to lose.

The half-time whistle blew
If England won they were through
There was a fifteen minute break
Could Northern Ireland give them a headache?

The Irish started the half very strong,
And a foul by Owen which was wrong
Their subs made a good impact on the game
Since then it was never the same.

They were into the last third of the match
And the Irish made a strong attack
Davis to Healy, past Robinson into the net
It looked like my uncle would win his bet.

The final whistle blew
And all England could do
Was stand and stare
As their dreams went up in the air.

Simon Mees (14)
Ballyclare High School

Butterflies

What is this?
Your heart pounds every so often,
It hurts to swallow
It's just him.

What is this?
You've never felt it before.
Is this normal?
It's just him.

What is this?
You have butterflies in your tummy
You smile for no real reason
It's just him.

What is this?
It's him.
He's the one giving you butterflies, making you smile.
It's just him.

What is this?
He's making your heart skip beats
This can't be safe
Maybe, it's just him.

Lauren Magowan (13)
Ballyclare High School

Healthy Heart

Have a healthy heart,
That is what they say,
I better not eat anymore tarts,
And eat more hay!
Go out for a run someday,
Maybe a day in May,
Or I will be brave,
And do it tomorrow,
So I won't end up in a grave,
And leave people with sorrow.

Kirsty Johnston (15)
Ballyclare High School

Hallowe'en

It's Hallowe'en, it's Hallowe'en
The moon is full and bright
And we shall see what can't be seen
On any other night.

Skeletons, ghosts and ghouls,
Grinning goblins fighting duels,
Werewolves rising from the gloom,
Witches on their magic brooms.

In masks and capes
We haunt the streets
And knock on doors
For trick and treat.

Tonight we are
The king and queen,
For oh, tonight
It's Hallowe'en.

Chris Grimley (14)
Ballyclare High School

Peaceful Skies

Prepared men
wEapons of mass destruction
fAmily waiting
Cries of pain
Early awakenings
battleFields
terrible circUmstances
cavaLry

no-man'S-land
everyone asKing, 'When will it end?'
artIllery
sErgeants
gaS attacks.

Joanna Davis (14)
Ballyclare High School

A Special Place!

Sometimes it's great to be around others,
And sometimes it's great to be alone!

When my thoughts are troubling me,
I have a special place to myself.

My place is quiet, there is little noise,
Just the sound of a stream trickling and an occasional duck.

My special place is out in the countryside,
It seems boring but it has something to hide.

The countryside is not just tractors and cows,
It has beautiful sights and natural sounds.

Amongst the tall grass and large trees,
It is my special place on the river's edge.

All the most natural and wonderful sounds can be heard,
Of small birds in flight, fish jumping and buzzards calling.

All the most wonderful sights can be seen,
Otters swimming, rabbits and hares hopping, all by the riverside.

Not a human, house or factory to be seen,
What a wonderful place to be.

Sun shining through the shade of the trees,
And a gentle breeze blowing, how peaceful for me.

Just me and nature there,
Parkgate is my special place.

Kyle Crawford (13)
Ballyclare High School

Hero

When you're down and out,
And you don't know what to do.
Just look inside,
And find the hero in you.

When you're feeling sad,
And your life's a mess.
Just rise up your hopes,
And the pain will be less.

All the hurt and pain,
Can go away.
Just hold your head up,
For another day.

When things go wrong,
And you don't know what to do.
Keep spirits high,
And start anew.

When you're all alone,
And everyone's gone.
Sing yourself
A happy song.

Be your own hero,
Just look inside.
Let all the hurt,
Wash away with the tide.

Just remember one little thing,
Your hero lies within.

Sarah-Jane Montgomery (13)
Ballyclare High School

Fighting To Stay Alive

When I look back in time,
At the times of my life,
I wonder why I'm here,
Fighting to stay alive.

Why did I come?
I am sure to die,
When I do, I hope that the angels -
Will fly with me to Heaven.

Fighting for my country,
Fighting for my family,
Missing them dearly,
Home is where I want to be.

Lots of men have died here,
From trench foot to phosgene gas
Many families shall grieve
When they find out the news.

Hopefully the war will end soon,
So that I can go back home.
So that I can leave this mayhem behind,
And go back to peace and quiet once more.

Laura French (15)
Ballyclare High School

'Tis True, 'Tis True

War is bad, 'tis true, 'tis true
Death occurs, 'tis true, 'tis true.
Bombs and gas, 'tis true, 'tis true
Bullets whizzing overhead, 'tis true, 'tis true.

People fighting till the end, 'tis true, 'tis true
Treachery happens, 'tis true, 'tis true
Destruction takes place, 'tis true, 'tis true
All this is true, 'tis true, this is true.

Michael Morrison (15)
Ballyclare High School

Universally Talking

At the edge there is a drop
Or is there a wall?
No one really knows
But the inventor of this space and all.

Will it stand the test of time?
It has lasted so long already.
When will be the end of the line?
But surely it is far too steady.

Some say it is always expanding,
Others say it is closing in on itself
Are they worthy of its understanding?
No one can compare with its wealth.

Man has tried to map it,
But this task is impossible,
No one could cover every bit,
Its boundaries unplausible.

Mark Wilson (16)
Ballyclare High School

Blindness

I have never ever, ever seen,
At least one thing that has been.
I've always smelt things a mile away,
Even if it has no smell.
I've always heard things no one else can hear,
Even if it's not near.
But this is very sad to say,
My sight will always be away.

Robyn Patton (12)
Ballyclare High School

Happy Hallowe'en

Hallowe'en, it's a wonderful time of year!
Celebration all around,
As the festive crowd cheer.

All in bright colours as they burst
It's a wonderful sight and for some it's a first,
But little do they know, Hallowe'en was caused by a curse.

One hundred years ago they say witches did fly so they
Sent fireworks to scare them into the sky.

These fireworks show so many colours and noises
Although some are quiet like whispering voices.

But louder is better say the firework makers
So we made some fireworks called Earthquakes.

But this old superstition stands no longer,
So enjoy the night and the beautiful sight.

Food and drink for the taking,
It's party time, so your head will be aching.

This event comes once a year,
So enjoy yourself, just watch and cheer.

Ross Glover (13)
Ballyclare High School

Off To The War

Off to battle our fearless soldiers go,
But to what fate
We will never know.

Will they be slaughtered, butchered or slain?
Will they rot in trenches
Their fighting in vain?

Will they be victorious, courageous and tough?
Fighting in fields
Having to go rough?

Andrew McCunn (14)
Ballyclare High School

Why We Fight

Why do we fight?
It is not for land - our supply is bountiful!
Why do we fight?
It is not for glory - there is none in war!
Why do we fight?
It is not for innocents - we kill more than we save!
Why do we fight?
It is not for freedom - we did not even ask them!
Why do we fight?
It is not for our loves - they are in no danger!
So why do we fight?
It is for black gold, dark and insidious as night.
So why do we fight?
It is for despots, as bad as those who they deposed.
So why do we fight?
It is because we are told to.

Daniel Barnett (13)
Ballyclare High School

Leaves - Haikus

Leaves are everywhere
On the ground and in tall trees
Thriving on moisture.

They float in the sky
Blowing softly in the breeze
All shapes and sizes.

Winter brings cold days
The leaves have fallen off trees
They are without life.

Summer brings warm days
Now the leaves are born again
Life fills their branches.

Rachael Stronge (15)
Ballyclare High School

Mountain Biking

Standing at the bottom
Waiting for your name
Then the marshal calls it
You bow your head like Stame.

You climb upon the chair lift
You're seeming pretty calm
Finally at the top
Helmet in your hand.

Finally at the top
You climb upon your bike
Putting on your helmet
Putting your goggles on tight.

Standing on the start line,
Ready to race,
Finally the whistle goes
You go down at a pace.

Flying over boulders
As if they were pebbles
The crowds are going wild,
You suddenly jam down on the pedals.

You're nearing the bottom
You see your time ticking away
You cross the line to take the lead
What an end to the day.

Matthew Jackson (14)
Ballyclare High School

The Real Meaning Of War

They call it the 'war'
But few know what that means
About the terror and fear
The brave soldiers have seen.

They felt pain and anguish
Their bodies lost and torn,
The meaning was different
For those who fought the 'war'.

The lucky stayed back
In the 'safety' of home,
While the less fortunate
Fought on unfamiliar loam.

The unforgettable scenes
Of the fight and the sound,
And the heartbreak of comrades
Lying still on the ground.

For those who survive the war goes on
In dreams both day and night,
The losses of both mind and limb
Constant reminder of the bloody fight.

Decades have passed
And the grass returned to green,
Save where the nodding scarlet poppies
Can now be seen.

Rachel McNeilly (14)
Ballyclare High School

The Christmas List

I wish I had an iPod
I wish I had a pet
I wish I had a horse so I could make a bet.

I wish I had an elephant
I wish I had a drink
I wish I had a little toy that is very square and pink.

I wish I had a girlfriend
I wish I had a football
I wish I could play rugby so I could ruck and mall.

I wish I had a scrambler
I wish I had a better noun
I wish I had a motorbike to ride around the town.

Please Santa, give me all these things.
                                    Thank you.

Ian Moxen (12)
Ballyclare High School

Fireworks

At last, Hallowe'en is here,
And people are full of cheer.

The first firework goes up, it is white,
As it goes up the noise causes a fright.

The second firework spirals up, it is green,
The colour of it, for miles can be seen.

The third firework burns the plastic coating through,
The colour of this Catherine wheel is blue.

The last firework is brown,
It shoots up and spirals down.

As the wind rose,
The festive celebration draws to a close.

Connor Gilpin (13)
Ballyclare High School

The Test

The day has come
I've got my good looks and reassurance from my mum.
I'm outside the class
Hopefully I'll get a grade that will pass
The teacher comes to let us in
Last minute revision to be put in
The papers are handed out
But I can't remember what it's about
Time is flying, it's not going well
The teacher stood up and said, 'Five minutes to the bell.'
In a panic I hurried,
When she said time was up, I was worried.
But I kept on going,
I still couldn't help knowing
That she would be coming
My brain was drumming
The end had come!
I went home to my mum!

David McDowell (13)
Ballyclare High School

Are You A Pop Idol?

Are you a pop idol
Or are you just idle?
Who thinks they can sing,
But really can't do anything.

You think you've got the X-Factor?
When really it sounds as if your throat is sore,
Holding the microphone trying to sing,
I'll tell you what, I'll show you the door.

Did you think you could have been in 'Popstars'?
If you had won you could have bought one of those fancy cars.
You could have, but you didn't win, your voice is so bad.
You should be stranded on Mars.

Chris Bew (13)
Ballyclare High School

Small Change

Like a newborn baby,
Shining and new,
Pressed out of the mint,
Stamped two thousand and two.

I soon realised,
This place was not my home,
When dispensed from the bank,
With the world left to roam.

I started my adventure
In an old lady's handbag,
But my mistress exchanged me,
For a lottery tag.

I had some good luck,
Which made people scream.
From one to a million pounds,
It seemed like a dream.

Life continued with many strangers,
From wallet to purse,
Where it was dirty and dark,
My life could not get much worse.

But my life was changed,
When a girl wished me away,
She threw me over her shoulder,
And hoped for a happy day.

I landed with a splash,
In a wishing well,
My life was at peace,
In a home where I now dwell.

Jennifer McBrien (13)
Ballyclare High School

Torn In Half

You're telling me your stories,
You're handing me a list,
You're giving me your point of view
But you never think of mine.
You tell me that you love me,
You say I ought to laugh
Why is it that you just can't see
That I am torn in half?
I try to laugh
But I am torn in half.

You say you can't be happy
With the way things used to be,
That things have changed for you now
So they must change for me.
You say that I'll get used to it,
That nothing ever lasts
Yes, that is your cause for it
But I am torn in half
No, nothing lasts
And I'm torn in half.

The whole world is divided
Seems set to break apart,
And now what you've decided
Is going to break my heart.

You made some vows a while ago
Before I came along,
But now I really need you
You think those vows are wrong.

You headed for a different life
You've got a brand new path
The things you've done cut like a knife
And leave me torn in half.
You've got a brand new path
But I'm torn in half.

Stuart McGreevy (13)
Ballyclare High School

Joshua

September 27th 2005, was set to be an extraordinary day
For nine months my mum had carried a load
Nine months feeling like a beached whale
But that Wednesday, Joshua McKeown was to be born
I came home from school
Happy and excited
But to our despair
Josh wasn't coming out
Ten days we had to wait
Suspense and excitement
Until . . .

October 7th 2005, was set to be an ordinary day
But the ringing of the phone at 3.30
Changed that
For nine months my mum had carried a load
Nine months of feeling like a balloon about to burst
That Friday
Joshua McKeown was born
It was my dad on the phone
Telling me the good news,
'Mum and baby are both fit and well,'
That night I went to visit
He was so small
So delicate
So harmless
I held him
He was so cute
My little brother.

Matthew McKeown (13)
Ballyclare High School

A Homeless Christmas - Haiku

Frozen turkey scraps
No chimney for Santa Claus
Endless nights of cold.

Jonathan Crone (13)
Ballyclare High School

10B

10B is my class
10B will not last
Because we make too much noise
But it isn't just all the boys
We play football every day
We all go to the fair every May
We all have fun and muck about
No one in our class would ever tout
When we break or shatter one of the lights
Harry and Connor often fight
We all laugh at Ross' jokes
Even when the teacher croaks
Grimley is the best goalkeeper
Sometimes we call him, 'The Grim Reaper'.
10B is always getting into trouble
And some day, someone, is going to burst our bubble
But until they do
We'll not rest
Because 10B is *simply the best!*

Ben Coote (13)
Ballyclare High School

Christmas Time

I love the feeling of Christmas time,
It gives people a chance to drink beer and wine.
The tree is up, the decorations are on,
The phone rings, it's my friend John.
He asks me, 'What do you want for Christmas?'
I reply, 'I haven't written my list.'
It's Christmas morning, a snowy day,
I've taught my new dog to sit and stay.
My new dog's name is Cooper,
My dinner's ready, it tastes super!

Ryan Wallace (13)
Ballyclare High School

My Dog

My dog is a springer spaniel,
She is called Meg,
She is brown and white
And sometimes bites.

Meg lives outside,
In a brown shed
She loves to beg for her dinner,
Which is fried eggs.

She loves her walks
At the forest.
She doesn't like other dogs,
And especially hates frogs.

She loves to swim and swim,
She loves the sea,
And she barks at the waves
My dog, Meg.

Mark Gault (13)
Ballyclare High School

Dracula

Dracula sits on the peak of a mountain
A castle made out of stone
When a human comes out he will shout,
'Here I come to suck your blood.'

He flies down as fast as an eagle
To express his evil

Then Van Helsing comes out
Holy water and all
He dips in his arrow, shoots and hits
And that is the end of Dracula!

Devan Brown (11)
Ballyclare High School

The Frog In The Kitchen

It was a cold and very wet morning,
I pulled myself out of bed
Got dressed and
Went down for breakfast
Where I saw something that made me scream off my head

I hadn't noticed it at first
And carried on as usual
In fact I
Nearly stepped on it
I don't know how it managed to get there at all

My brother was the one who spotted it
Just lying there on the floor
I jumped up
Onto my chair
And started to scream even more

We didn't know if it was living or dead
Until it moved around
My dad was
Away to his work
Leaving us to sort this thing on the ground

My mum hates frogs as much as me
This was creating such a fuss
My brother
Refused to take it out
I think he was as scared as us

We decided to use a brush and shovel
I was still on the chair
My mum ended
Up taking it out
It really gave us a scare!

Rachel McMillan (13)
Ballyclare High School

One Little Witch

One little witch,
Watched one little watch,

Her family thought she'd gone crazy,
Agreed mother who danced with baby,

That one little witch,
That watched one little watch,
Was making a great big spell,

Frogs' heads and dogs' heads,
All sprinkled with cheese,

Some garlic and rhubarb oh please,

In went a cat, a rat and a bat,
All carefully tinted with garnish,

Her mother said, 'Oh dear, oh my!
What has my child done with the varnish?'

Hannah Welshman (11)
Ballyclare High School

Autumn

Once again it's that time of year,
When winter is near
The leaves on the trees,
Are slowly changing,
To colours like orange
And green is fading.

October is coming near,
Hallowe'en is in sight
The fireworks we can hear
The sparklers are alight.

Animals harvesting food,
Ready for hibernation
And bringing it back to their
Secret location.

Christina Turkington (12)
Ballyclare High School

Secret Love

You speak to me every day
And still you do not know,
That I have always loved you,
But cannot let it show
I wish that you would take me,
With you to the 'formal'.
Should my heart be aching?
Is this feeling normal?
My aching heart is burning,
Burning with desire.
I want to be with you,
Only you can quench this fire,
That's raging in my heart.
It makes my body quake.
Every time I'm with you,
My lips will start to shake.
This love is unbelievable,
A feeling quite unique.
I sit beside you every day
Just to hear you speak.
I lie upon my bed at night,
And cry myself to sleep
I've never felt this way before,
This love is just too deep.
I want to tell you how I feel,
I can't cope with this pain.
I can't keep all this bottled up,
It's driving me insane!

Holly Steele-Nicholson (15)
Ballyclare High School

Luke!

Dad: Luke! Sweep the walls!
Luke: What shall I sweep them with?
Dad: Use the broom!
Luke: But the broom handle is broken.
Dad: Then fix it!
Luke: What shall I fix it with?
Dad: The curtain rod!
Luke: But the curtain rod is too long.
Dad: Then cut it!
Luke: What should I cut it with?
Dad: Use the saw.
Luke: Where's the saw?
Dad: It's in the garage!
Luke: But the garage is too messy.
Dad: Then clean it!
Luke: What should I clean it with?
Dad: Use the broom!
Luke: But the broom handle is broken!

Luke Johnston (12)
Ballyclare High School

The Countryside

The countryside is my favourite place to be
With so much picturesque scenery
Lush green fields seem to stretch for miles
Old trees gnarled with age standing tall
The scent of beautiful blossoms drift through the air
I watch as farmers gather in their crops
Before the harsh winter begins and evenings drop
Long walks with my dad are memories I will always treasure
The countryside is not only the home of birds and animals
It is also my home
And where I never want to leave.

Orla Carmichael (13)
Ballyclare High School

If Only I Had My Senses

I have lost my senses oh dear
Oh well I'll just have a beer
If only I could see
I wouldn't have eaten a bee
If only I could talk
I wouldn't have asked for a sock
If only I could feel
I wouldn't have got an eel
If only I could taste
I wouldn't have ate toxic waste
If only I could hear
I would have found Miss Grear.
Lost
Miss Grear
Reward 1,000,000.

James Hall (11)
Ballyclare High School

Basketball's My Favourlte Sport

Basketball's my favourite sport
I dribble up and down the court
The ball comes bouncing off my toes
And beans the teacher on the nose.

He stumbles back and grabs his nose
And hits the wall and down he goes,
All the players stop and stare
They've never heard the teacher swear!

With no one playing anymore
I grab the ball, I shoot, I score!
I love this game, it's so much fun
The teacher cried, but we still won!

Alastair Hunter (11)
Ballyclare High School

War

Blaring sun, pouring rain, killing guns
Loss of life, loss of limbs, glory to the man
Who dies for king and country.

Amputees, drill sergeants roar, artillery shell
Blast the enemy down deep to Hell
Fear not the guns or bayonet but fear
The fear that you fear so well.

But why the death and fear and terror
Where men live to die and are trained
To kill and be killed?
Is this war finally the end?
No more fighting, death or killing.
The sergeant, 'Fears do not win wars.
So do not fear that pillbox, it's short
Work for artillery shell.'

We're not the soldiers of France
Or India, we're not the saviours of WWI,
We're modern day soldiers in the killing ground
That is and always will be war.

Nicholas Wray (14)
Ballyclare High School

Autumn

A bsolutely wonderful
U niversal, it happens everywhere!
T rees, most lose their leaves
U biquitous - it's everywhere
M anifest - you can't miss it
N ippy, it's very cold!

Chloe Pickering (11)
Ballyclare High School

Marching To War

As they marched down the dusty track,
Guns over their shoulders like heavy socks.
Boots shimmering in the light,
'Will we get here before night?'
Marching forth as the campsites they see,
An ongoing war out at sea.
Faces wondering if it was their friend,
Hoping that it wouldn't be the end.
They don't know what lies ahead,
Months of war, millions of dead
Fathers, sons, husbands all lose,
Many will die in the Holocaust.
Killing people they will do,
Never knowing a nightmare would come true.
But they will fight with glory and with pride,
Their enemy weapons by their side.
Soon more than half of this troop won't be here anymore,
And the major will have to send for more.
Young men they will be just the others,
They all had family, friends and mothers.
I suppose that's the price to pay,
For being a brave soldier all the way.

Hannah Coleman (15)
Ballyclare High School

School

S cience, maths and English too
C an sometimes confuse you
H istory, French and German too
O n weekdays may not amuse you
O verall don't forget, try your best to enjoy it
L ive, love and learn. It's the best days of your life.

Leah Spiers (11)
Ballyclare High School

The Pride Of Our Country

A wife looks out at the snow,
Where her husband is,
Does anyone know?

Off to war,
Thousands of men,
Just wondering when, O when?

Over the trenches they go,
Fathers and sons,
Mown down by guns.

The winter passes in the trenches
The weather hot,
The smell of rot.

Death and destruction everywhere,
The leaders at home,
Do they even care?

Then comes that dreaded letter,
Families devastated,
Will it ever get better?

The pride of our country,
Gone off to war,
Most are dead, near and far.

Thousands are dead,
Cities in dust,
But fight on for our country we must!

Amy Lockhart (14)
Ballyclare High School

A Long Time Ago

A long time ago
When the world was
Covered with snow.
Nothing could grow
And no rivers could flow.

A long time ago
There were people
We will never see
But we can all
Aspire to be.

A long time ago
And suffered many a blow
But are historic figures
That we all know.

A long time ago
To new places people decided to go.
They were further than a stone-throw
But are all places we all know.

How did they survive?
What was it like?
It's fun looking back
To see what our world
Was like.

Gareth Armstrong (12)
Ballyclare High School

The Teacher's Dead

It's raining, it's pouring,
This class is boring.
The teacher is snoring.
Hit her on the head with a loaf of bread.
And now she's dead,
Put her in the shed and let's call for Mr Edd.

Christopher Davis (12)
Ballyclare High School

Who Am I?

Who am I?
My mum thinks I'm fantastic,
My dad sees me as his heir,
My baby sister thinks I'm her hero,
My older sister doesn't care.

My granny thinks I'm her favourite grandson,
'Cause I'm the only one.
My teacher thinks I work hard
My friend sees me as a bit of fun.

With all these different words
In my head,
No wonder I feel confused,
Who am I? What a question!
At least it keeps me amused!

Ryan Cochrane (13)
Ballyclare High School

Love Is Blind

Love is blind
How could I not see from first sight
You were there for me through everything
In times of need you were always there.

Love is blind
I was blinded by hate and blame
I lost you once, hopefully never again
I hope you would agree.

Love was blind
The chance was there and now it's gone
We have gone our separate ways
Never together, maybe some things aren't meant to be.

Andrew Kelly (15)
Ballyclare High School

Earthquake

To my one true love who I could not save,
One last cross over one lost grave,
I wonder how your last hours were spent,
And where your smiles and laughter went,
Others stand over your grave and weep,
But memories of you in my heart I'll keep,
So I may stand and smile through my tears,
As your love echoes down through all my years,
I know that you are not truly dead,
You have merely gone before,
And are waving back at me,
From some distant shore,
Although quakes and shocks may rip the ground,
My soul, my heart, will be safe and sound,
Buildings may no longer bend and fall apart,
And sutures may repair my broken heart,
For I know that at my end,
I will be with you, my one true love, my darling friend.

Lauryn Scott (16)
Ballyclare High School

Thoughts Of Autumn

Cool misty mornings
Cobwebs decorated with tiny drops of water.
Red-berried bushes complimented with evergreen leaves
Low lying branches laden with apples
Bare branchy trees starting to appear.
Fluttering and tumbling vivid coloured leaves.
Ground covered with leafy quilts
Little mounds of green, rusty, gold and brown asking to be kicked.
Young children enjoying new welly boots
Scarves in every colour on show.
Darkening afternoons.
People everywhere eager to get in their home.

Rachel Herron (12)
Ballyclare High School

Brothers-In-Arms

He landed frightened
On his own
Drenched by weakness and fear.

Bullets whizzing like the fireworks he had known as a child
Vibrating round his ears.
The white sands
Splattered red.

Stumbling over dying men
Forced to move by those behind him,
His courage left at home many months before,
Hidden away in a drawer in his room so no one would know
                                              it had gone.

Maybe he heard the bullet, which hit him
Maybe he didn't.
I hoped he hadn't as I nursed him in my arms,
And lowered him to the Normandy sand.
My brother-in-arms.

Jane Croskery (13)
Ballyclare High School

Snowy Christmas

I love it when the snow comes down,
White, white all around.
On no one's face is there a frown
With the lovely snowy sound.

The weather makes you cheery and merry,
Children throwing snowballs,
People eating Christmas cake and berries,
Hanging stockings at the fireplace.

Louisa Johnston (13)
Ballyclare High School

Christmas Time

When it comes near Christmas
It's so much fun
Excitement, happiness and joy
Thinking about opening your favourite toy.

On the eve that special day
You can hardly sleep
Tossing and turning all night long
And humming along to your favourite Christmas song.

When the morning comes
You jump up and run on down
You tear through the wrapping paper quick
And eat until you feel quite sick.

Once the day finally ends
A sad feeling begins
That having to wait a whole year for that night
It went by so quick, it gave me quite a fright!

Hannah McClure (12)
Ballyclare High School

Cake

I love to bake a cake
It can be fun to make
And you'd be surprised
At how short a time it takes.

Coffee cake,
Chocolate cake
Any cake
It's just fun to bake.

Zara Taylor (15)
Ballyclare High School

My 'Wee' Joe

Once a day
I would go
Down to the field
To see my 'wee' Joe

When I would tell him
'Bout my day at school
He'd tell me that,
I was a fool.

Then he'd tell me
What he did at school
And I would gasp
And say, 'You rule.'

You know what this is saying
Come on, you can guess
He was popular, I was not,
But he still thought I was the best.

I loved him dearly
And he loved me too
But he's gone now
Forever and I feel so blue.

Hannah McClay (11)
Ballyclare High School

Pencil Neck

There was once a boy called Cecil
Who liked to chew on his pencil,
It got stuck down his throat,
And boy did he choke,
And now he is left with a whistle.

Peter Kennedy (12)
Ballyclare High School

My Dream

Football is my hobby
I give it my all
The crowd go wild
Every time I touch the ball
I can't believe it we've scored a goal
We're going top of the League
We've finally made the breakthrough
We've put Everton 20th
We've put Chelsea 2nd
Now we're first
And in dreamland now
We have done it
We've won the League
We are Liverpool
We're the best team
I've woken up now
It's all been a dream
I look at the scores
We're winning 2-0
Chelsea are getting beat
My dream has come true
We've won the League
I hope that I dream we win the treble
Then we'll win that too!

James Conville (12)
Ballyclare High School

In The Morning

Morning has come, the day has begun.
Darkness breaks, up comes the sun.
I get out of bed, I wash my face.
Time to quicken up my pace.
I'm going to be late for the bus.
I really hate all this fuss.

Sarah McConnell (12)
Ballyclare High School

School

School can be fun or school can be wick'
Whatever you make it, there's no time to act thick
Maths is plain boring with decimals and fractions
And funny old sub-teachers who can't do subtractions
English is all right; the teachers are wacky
Except when they make you read Shakespeare, it's batty!
History is quite fun, the Romans are classy
But Henry VIII and his wives are just ghastly!
French is a laugh when it's bonjour and au revoir
But when you're into your verbs like choisir and avoir
It gets too confusing and makes matters dire
Geography is great fun when it's countries and maps
Then when you do weathering, your head swells like a bap
RE's fantastic, the teachers are cool
The commandments are good fun but make some people drool
HE teachers are fussy and boss you around
But the cooking is great and it comes in big mounds
Tech's really boring when you're taking down notes
Whilst the practicals give time for drilling, filing and jokes
German is easy if you know what to do
Learning genders and verbs like spielen and du
Art's not too bad, the teachers are rare
They make you draw pictures, especially of pears
Music is fab fun, the teachers throw tantrums
We write our own songs and play national anthems
Games is the best, playing hockey and netball
But your hair gets messed up when you try not to fall.

Suzanne James (12)
Ballyclare High School

I Hate Thunder!

When I snuggle down to sleep,
Above my head I hear you creep.
I hear you moan, I hear you groan,
When I am lying all alone.

You seem so distant yet so close,
I don't know what I fear the most.
Is it the grumble? Is it the tumble,
Or could it be the dreadful rumble?

I really, really hate to say,
I do not like you, night or day.
You really are an awful pain,
I've even started to hate the rain.

Many people feel like me,
Because you make us feel so 'wee'.
Have you guessed or do you wonder,
'Cause it's true that *I hate thunder!*

Rebecca Bonar (12)
Ballyclare High School

Rugby

Rugby is my favourite sport
I play it every day.
The position I play is scrum-half.
I love it when I win.
I play for Ballyclare High School
And for Ballyclare rugby club as well.
We are the best in our league,
I am the captain of my team.
I have to shout a lot.

Marc Logan (12)
Ballyclare High School

Tomorrow Never Comes

I wish that tomorrow
I could go out and
Buy myself a new mobile.
I wish that tomorrow
I could buy myself
A luxurious yacht and
Sail around Europe.
I wish that tomorrow
I didn't have to go
To school and that
I could shop all day.

I wish that tomorrow
Everyone in the world
Will be at rest,
With no wars or sudden deaths,
With every living day,
All we can do is hope and pray.

Sonia Crawford (13)
Ballyclare High School

Lost Your Senses

What if you had lost your senses?
You would be painting cheese and eating fences.
What if you had lost your sight?
You couldn't read or you couldn't write.
If only I could hear or touch.
Last night I slept in the rabbit hutch.
If only I could smell or taste.
I wouldn't have eaten the wallpaper paste.
Sometimes I feel like I can see,
Or maybe it's because I ate the bumblebee!

Mark Rowntree (12)
Ballyclare High School

The Pest

There was a little fly,
Buzzing through the air
He landed on my leg
And decided to settle himself there.
To make himself comfy
Was a really big mistake
Because I wanted to squash him flat
Like a mini pancake.
So I grabbed the Daily Mirror
And rolled it up tight,
Boy, was this little chap
Going to get a *big* fright
So I pulled back my arm
Got ready,
Fire!
Splat!
And that was the end of that.

Suzanne Wilson (12)
Ballyclare High School

School!

Why do we go?
To school
Even if the winds blow
To school
Even if the snow falls
To school
Even if our nose runs
To school
Especially on a Monday morning
To school.

Rebecca Rankin (12)
Ballyclare High School

Football Is . . .

Football is a passion
A passion for the game
The only game where you can see
A grown man go insane.

Football is a team sport
Eleven men playing as one
It is not just the striker who scored the goal
But the whole team plays as one.

Football is a challenge
A challenge for all the team
With injuries and relegations
The tally of goals can be lean.

Football is the greatest
The greatest sport on Earth
To win the World Cup's a dream
For every footballer from birth.

Paul White (13)
Ballyclare High School

Snowdrops

White little petals
Hanging in the breeze
Murmuring to each other
Some folk say they are whispering,
'The winter's almost over.'
Sparkling in the frost
Round the old oak tree
Watching all the people
Drinking cups of tea.

Ellie Watson (11)
Ballyclare High School

If The World Was Made Of Sweets!

If the world was made of sweets,
The land would be made of marshmallows,
When you'd walk it would smell so sweet,
And you could eat it as a treat,
If the world was made of sweets!

If the world was made of sweets,
The clouds would be candyfloss,
Instead of white they would be pink,
And if you sat on them you wouldn't sink,
If the world was made of sweets!

If the world was made of sweets,
The trees would be chocolate rolls,
So if you chopped the tree in two,
Cream would flow out just for you,
If the world was made of sweets!

If the world was made of sweets,
The beaches would be sherbet dip,
So if you got sand in your food,
You wouldn't go off in a huffy mood,
If the world was made of sweets!

Laura Thompson (11)
Ballyclare High School

Holidays

H olidays are great, they get you away
O ver the seas and to Lanzarote Bay
L ying in the sunshine, the warmth on my skin
 I don't want to leave here - it would be such a sin
D uring the day it is all 'get up and go'
A t night it is so different - the pace becomes slow
Y ikes! It is Tuesday - our last day is here,
S o let's get our brochures out and book for next year!

Nicola Lennon (12)
Ballyclare High School

What Should I Be?

Should I be an astronaut and fly up to space,
Or should I be a teacher and boss the human race,
Oh what, oh what should I be?

Maybe I could be an author and write exciting books,
Or I could be a model with my lovely looks,
Oh what, oh what should I be?

I could win the X-Factor,
Or be a famous actor,
Oh what, oh what should I be?

Should I be an inventor and invent new things,
Or I could be a goldsmith and make lovely rings,
Oh yes, oh yes, I know what I want to be,
But you will have to wait a little longer to see.

Sarah Carmichael (11)
Ballyclare High School

First Love

F rom a cardboard box you came
I nto my life
R emote control came with you too;
S kybox came at a reduced price
T V, you are the love of my life!

L ove is not strong enough for our bond
O nly you can comfort me in bad times
V icar of Dibley, Friends, ER . . .
E veryone loves you for who you are!

Amy McConnell & Catherine Crawford (16)
Ballyclare High School

Liverpool!

Liverpool is the best team ever,
Man United can't beat them - not now, not never!
We all know who is the best,
It's the men in the red vests!

With Rafael Benitez and Rick Parry,
The Liverpool fans are as happy as Larry
They always try not to lose a game,
To win the European Cup is their aim!

The greatest moment that I can recall,
Was when Liverpool beat Chelsea for the ball,
They showed great talent and plenty of skill,
And the final score, Liverpool one, Chelsea nil!

With their mighty army of reds,
They will put all the other teams to bed,
Our unstoppable captain Stevie G,
Will lead us to victory, just wait and see!

Now my poem has come to an end,
I've driven Man U and Chelsea fans around the bend!

Shauna-Lee Warwick (11)
Ballyclare High School

Hallowe'en

H appy children's faces
A ll the children, all dressed up
L ate nights
L ots of children go to the dentist
O ther children are dressing up scary
W hen Hallowe'en is coming, I get excited
E veryone is out trick or treating
E very shop is sold out of sweets
N ight sky is decorated with fireworks.

Laura Fekkes (11)
Ballyclare High School

Nanny Brown

Nanny Brown
From Portadown
Not from Ballyboly

Said Nanny Brown
From Portadown,
'I really do like gravy
I like it sweet
With lots of meat
And splashed with a drop of wine.'

Nanny Brown
She had a frown
Upon her face, one day
I asked her why
And then she cried
'I've lost my tin of gravy.'

Jill Morrow (12)
Ballyclare High School

On The Phone

It's Sophie on the phone again,
I pretend to feel happy at the news, wishing I was
Somewhere else.
Munching on some crisps I mumble with enthusiasm,
While I stroke my parrot (I've never had a blue parrot before)
Sophie is still ranting on, dreaming of being in Spain right now,
In the glorious sun.
Goodbye Sophie
You've just bored the parrot and me to death!

Megan Patterson (13)
Ballyclare High School

My Granda

My granda's head is like an egg
His mouth's like a red liquorice lace
His eyes are the shape of almonds
And they're as blue as the sky above
When he walks, he's like a snail
It's hard to keep at his pace!
I love my granda all the same
And I would never change him for the world!

Sarah Shannon (12)
Ballyclare High School

Paddy

I want to drive Paddy,
He's 22 ton
When I asked my daddy,
He said, 'No chance. None!'

So I drove Molly,
That was fine.
And then with Polly,
On Paddy, we would dine.

I then got to drive Headway,
Unable to see where I was going.
Boy that was a good day,
Until I fell and then from my eyes tears were flowing.

One day hopefully quite soon,
And trying not to break anyone's limb
Maybe just once in a blue moon,
I'm going to drive him.

Margaret Dunlop (13)
Ballymena Academy

The Morning After The Battle

The morning dew has fallen,
The soldiers are lying unmoving,
Have lost their bloody pollen,
The birds sing a song of sorrow.

This war is costing nothing but lives,
The few survivors limp and amble,
The bullets are flying like knives
Piercing the flesh of noble men.

This bloodshed is needless,
There must be a moral solution,
To prevent this bloody mess,
It represents a failure to listen.

The leaders of this world can't see,
What the consequences are,
And what they're making this world to be,
Why can't we all just get along . . .

Just to live in peace and harmony?

Adam Henry (12)
Ballymena Academy

Little Birds

Little birds flying through the air
Causing us to stop and stare
Busily they build their nests
To hatch their eggs away from pests!

The wind doth blow from east to west
But their nests are high and free from stress
The little chicks are hatching soon
In the early hours of the afternoon

The mothers carry to their young
Worms and slugs for everyone
When all are fed, there's not a cheep
For Mother's young are fast asleep.

Emma McKeown (13)
Ballymena Academy

Young Writers - POP! Co Antrim

What Are The Stars?

The stars are like the blinking eyes
Of a taxi, beating down the back streets.
They are the flickering street lights
Shining on a dark street.
They are fidgeting bubbles
Popping and fizzing in a bottle of cola.

The stars are one hundred starfish
Wriggling in the deep, dark sea.
They are a billion dots on a black page
Made with a glow-in-the-dark pen.
They are a collection of small silver coins
Lying snug in a blue velvet purse.

The stars are the flashlights of a Girl Guides' camp
Gleaming into the darkness.
They are the glare of feline headlamps
As he slinks silently round the corner.
They are a silvery dusting of frost in the morning
Left in the night by a visitor.

The stars are luminous fireworks
Going *bang!* in the midnight sky.
They are twinkling fairy lights
On a cheery Christmas tree.
They are the flecks of foam
Dancing on an angerod occan.

Up there, far above us,
Glittering stars galore,
Wish upon a star tonight,
And you'll have no worries for evermore.

Sheenagh Aiken (13)
Ballymena Academy

Summer

Summer is a feast for the senses,
A time of fun,
And laughter,
It is the most exciting time of the year.

The sweet taste of honey,
The taste of cold ice cream, cooling you down,
It is the most delicious time of the year.

The beautiful birds singing their heavenly hymns,
The harsh sunlight beating down,
It is the most beautiful time of the year.

The sweet smell of the flowers smiling sweetly,
The smell of freshly cut grass,
It is the most scented time of the year.

The time of families and the seaside,
It truly is the best time of the year.

Ben Monteith (12)
Ballymena Academy

Tsunami

The giant wave slams down,
On the now deserted ground,
Cries of help are being heard,
As the news soon spreads across the world.

Rescue workers are coming now,
Through the dirt and rubble they plough,
Searching through the streets,
To see the devastating sights their eyes meet.

Rebuilding the town comes at great cost,
But will never replace the loved ones lost,
They can just hope that never again,
They feel the same anger, sadness and pain.

Rachel Mairs (12)
Ballymena Academy

My Gran Is Turning 75

My gran is turning 75,
Yet she still looks fit and alive,
She doesn't look a day over 50,
I think, for an old girl, she's pretty nifty.

She's still young you see,
But I don't think her hips would agree,
She doesn't like turning old,
And hates the thought of an old folks' fold.

She drives around in her little red car,
And she's not afraid to give it some power,
She goes so fast she would give you a fright,
And soon your hair would be just as white.

I don't think she will ever slow down,
Or ever stop acting the clown,
She is a wee bit slower to dance and jive,
But remember, my gran is 75.

John Andrew (12)
Ballymena Academy

That Night

I was there on that night
When everything went right
England came to knock us down
But they left with a frown
Laurie's men gave their all
And watched the millionaires fall
Sven didn't know what to do
So all his substitutes on he threw
For all the use they would be
He might as well have brought on you and me
A night like this may never come again
But this feeling will always remain!

Jenny Dickson (12)
Ballymena Academy

The Black Cat!

I have a cat and her name is Finn,
And when I'm out she's always in,
She loves to eat and sleep during the day,
But if it's night she'll want you to play.

She loves to eat spiders and daddy-long-legs too,
But when Finn's angry, she will try to scratch you.
Sometimes I tell her off when she's bad,
And then her face looks really sad.

She loves people to stroke her fur,
And if you do, she'll lick you and purr.
Finn's very quiet and very shy
And Finn has lovely, big green eyes.

One day Finn got soot all over her paws
And put tiny paw prints all over the walls.
But although Finn likes to make a mess,
I still think that my cat is the best!

Chloe Bartley (12)
Ballymena Academy

Sheep

The animal that defines Ballymena,
Great little clouds that have four legs,
With no common sense even at old age
Ponder all day and eat constantly,
Like little lawnmowers, only without the petrol.
So perhaps they are saving money in a way.
A long *baa* . . . ! wakes you in the morning.
In the field where one goes they all follow,
Some people think their heads are hollow.
When it's time to have them sheared,
They kick up a fuss,
When it's all done they leave in disgust.
But funny enough, I like the little balls of fluff.

Matthew Hill (13)
Ballymena Academy

Autumn

As you walk along the ground,
You hear the wind howling all around,
You feel the coldness on your face,
You had better pick up the pace.

As you walk along the ground,
You step on something with a crackling sound,
You see it lying, what must it be?
It is leaves, fallen from a tree.

As you walk along the ground,
You stop and hear the different sounds,
You hear the birds which sing so sweet,
And you start to tap to the beat.

As you walk along the ground,
You wonder about the things you've found,
You pause, and think about it all,
Yes, you're right, it's autumn's fall.

Zoë McLees (12)
Ballymena Academy

The Hedgehog's Lament

I hide in fear
For tomorrow winter comes,
Flowers die, colour gone
The ground white with snow.
This land becomes grey
I have to sleep
Through the winter long.
Nowhere to go, I have to stay,
In a nest made of leaves.
When spring comes, I will be glad
In my head I think, *hooray!*

Sarah Close (12)
Ballymena Academy

First Day Of School

My hair is sweaty,
Head sore, legs are heavy,
There's dirt on my blazer already,
School's vanilla jelly,
I'm scared, but to the eye I look neat and ready,
To go to class,
But I keep on forgetting what I've learnt now,
The teacher's cross, she has a frown,
She's screaming now,
I'm nervous, beaming now,
The class is loud,
My heart is racing,
My head feels like a drum,
I look at my watch,
Sweat runs down my brow,
Bell rings, I breathe a sigh,
Class is out, freedom at last.

Andrew McCloy (13)
Ballymena Academy

Northern Ireland

Northern Ireland are the best
They are better than the rest
When Healy gets the ball
Unless he's fouled he will not fall.

Up the right there is Gillespie,
He always can produce a recipe.
On the left there is Elliott or Brunt
They're always sharp, never blunt.

In defence is Aaron Hughes
He'll defend so they'll never lose.
Up front is Jimmy Quinn
He'll set up goals so they win.

Adam Hunter (12)
Ballymena Academy

A School Day

Oops, it's school and I'm not feeling too well,
Ah well, I guess I can't go.
OK, spin round ten times, dizzy, check,
Punch myself in chest really hard, sick, check,
Now I'm definitely sick.

'Muuuum! I'm really, really, really sick.'
'Really? Let's see your fever then.'
'Uh, no. If I put anything in my mouth I'll be sick.
I'd better stay in my bed with some hot chocolate.'

'Well, what's the matter with you then?'
'Well, where do I start? I'm dizzy,
My stomach is really, really sore and so is my chest,
And my eyes are sore and sticky.'
'Right, I get the point.'

'It's a pity you are sick today.'
'Why? What's happening today?'
'Oh nothing, it's just that it's Saturday and . . .'
'Saturday! Well, I'm well now and I'm off to play. Bye!'

Andrew Gawn (12)
Ballymena Academy

The Solemn Tree

A silent soldier stands in my garden,
Rooted there since before I was born
His armour a coat of leaves
His weapons the pointing branches
Stretched out to defend his territory
The gnarled trunk surrounds him
Insulating against cold and heat,
But in winter his leafless fingers
Plead with the grey black sky
For spring's renewing warmth
When once again he will stand
Tall and proud, undefeated in battle.

Alan MacPherson (13)
Ballymena Academy

School Things

Pencil case, school bag, locker key,
Corridor, homework, master's degree,
Teachers, staff room, lunch detentions,
Grammar, essays, comprehensions

Square root, graphs and multiplication,
Mixed fractions, confusion total
Frustration!
Atoms, reactions, periodic tables,
Forces, electricity, grounded cables.

Great kings and queens start revolutions,
Wars, gory battles and executions,
Rivers, mountains, diversifications,
Industry, transport and rock formations.

Moses, the Bible, the Crucifixion,
Preaching the good news, the Benediction.
Goals, pitches, socks and shin guards,
Netball, tennis court, he's got a red card.

Francais, bleu, cheveux et soeur,
Oiseau, chat et bonjour monsieur
Pizzara, amigo, levantaos,
Hola, lapiz, por favor sentaos

Projects, research, lengthy homework,
Exhaustion, boredom, going berserk,
TV, relax, rest your head,
Finish, end and go to bed.

Charlotte Kane (12)
Ballymena Academy

My Pet Dragon's Visit To School

One day I thought it would be cool,
To bring my pet dragon to school.
I tried to put him in the car,
But the car wouldn't go very far.
I thought that we could use the bus,
But the driver wouldn't let us.
By this time we were really late,
I had to chase him to the gate.

I showed him to the teacher
And she cried, 'What's that creature?'
All the children gathered around,
Suddenly, my dragon couldn't be found.
I ran down the corridor from room to room,
And then I found him eating a broom.
I shouted, 'What are you doing?'
But he just kept on chewing.

By now the caretaker was in a rage,
We had to put my dragon in a cage.
My dragon is very hard to tire,
And then he set his cage on fire.
I ran for the hose,
While he stood in a pose.
I probably shouldn't have brought him to school,
My teacher and I agree it wasn't very cool.

Adam McKeown (11)
Ballymena Academy

The Poppy Field

There's a place called the Somme, which used to be a battlefield.
It's now a peaceful area, covered with a sea of red.
Not the red of blood where thousands fought and died
But a sea of poppies, growing in the summer sun.

Bullets and bombs exploded, to the left, right and centre.
For seven long days and nights they fell.
And if there was a Hell on Earth, then this was the place,
But on that fateful hour at seven-thirty in the morning
A chilling silence swept the area as soldiers went over the front.

They all lined up beside each other, father, son and brother,
With a blast of a whistle they all moved forward.
Some threw grenades as they made their advance
To clear the barb wire for the big push.

The enemy appeared and saw them coming,
Hundreds and thousands of brave young men.
They opened up with their heavy guns
On the unsuspecting, brave young men.
Many were injured and many more died
As they advanced towards the enemy lines.

They are now remembered on the eleventh of November
The day the war ended to end all wars.
The Earl Haig Fund collects for all the war injured,
Known to you and me as the 'Poppy Appeal'.

Ryan McFarland (12)
Ballymena Academy

122   *Young Writers - POP! Co Antrim*

Summer Dying Fast

The summer is dead
For another year
Everything is gone
It has disappeared

It went so fast
And was good fun
The sea and the beach
And especially the sun

The first month of June
Was wasted in school
When we could have had fun
Playing by the pool

It's hard not to feel
Angry about this all
I could have used this time
To have fun with a ball

Although I'm not happy
It's not all bad
Summer will be back again
No need to be sad.

Jordan Allen (13)
Ballymena Academy

Autumn/Winter

All the leaves are falling,
Animals are going into hibernation,
As the time goes back an hour,
The sky is getting darker even quicker,
Winter is coming in fast,
As the log fires heat us up,
The house is really cosy,
It's the time for lots of snow,
With snowball fights and snowmen,
Winter is my favourite season.

Aaron Fry (12)
Ballymena Academy

Galloping

My favourite place on a summer's day
Is sitting astride my pony,
On the golden sand of Portstewart Strand
On a windy day that's sunny.

With the crashing waves on one side
And the sand dunes on the other,
The open beach stretching ahead,
It's a feeling like no other.

As I stand up on the stirrups
My pony senses fun,
He dances and prances about,
He just wants to run, run, run!

I squeeze his sides and off we go
The feeling I can't describe
Exhilaration, coursing through my veins
What a wonderful, wonderful ride.

Panting and puffing noisily
I slow him to a trot,
I let him cool off in the waves
'Cause he is very, very hot.

As I load my pony into his box,
I finally come back to reality
I'm already planning my next ride
I hope, in the same locality.

Shannon Tella (12)
Ballymena Academy

Earthquake

It has just hit,
Teams from across the world,
Trying to find any bit
Of life.
Is there anyone to be saved?

The screams are all you can hear,
All the sniffer dogs are out,
Anything to the trained ear.
Anyone to be saved?

All the buildings go down,
Many children are in school,
Anything up in town?
Anyone to be saved?

It's a sore sight to see,
Many on the helicopter,
A lot more wish they could be,
Anyone to be saved?

The despair is depressing me,
The aftershocks too,
I wish I could be
A help.
How many are saved?

David Headden (12)
Ballymena Academy

Save The Trees

A mighty trunk and whispering leaves,
We depend a lot on trees
We need the wood for building, fine,
We need the beech, the oak, the pine
We need it for the paper, white
Upon which, we humans write.
In fact we even need them to breathe
Yes, we depend a lot on trees.
But soon, the trees will disappear
Man bears his axe and sheds no tear
He cuts them down and down and down
The trees come crashing to the ground
And soon we'll have nothing you see,
Because we'll have murdered all the trees.
There'll be no wood for building, fine
There'll be no beech, no oak, no pine
There'll be no more paper white,
Upon which we humans write.
In fact we won't be able to breathe
So come on folks,
Save the trees!

Andrew Deaney (14)
Ballymena Academy

Tony's 'Children'

As student fees keep rising
Gordon Brown keeps smiling,
Whilst students pay the heavy price
That will lay on their shoulders for the rest of their lives,
Parents heave a sigh
That would weaken the bridge that lies,
Who cares about our future careers?
Whilst Tony's children are expensively reared
On public schooling and the rest,
We all find ourselves in financial mess.

Sophie Glass (17)
Ballymena Academy

The Perfect Pet

My friend once bought me a newt
He said it was very cute
But when it came and I looked
It was nothing but minute.

My friend next bought me a mole
He said he'd taught it to roll
Age, it seemed, had took its toll
As all it could do was snore.

My friend then bought me a hawk
He said that it could talk
With it I went for a walk
But it soon took off like a shot.

My friend then bought me a cat
He said it was a mini acrobat
It loved to chase after rats
One time, though, it never came back.

Scott Goodrich (13)
Ballymena Academy

Tree Poem!

As I walk along beside the trees,
Their long branches seem to reach out for me.
Some of them are there a long time,
Some others are as skinny as a vine.
Most of them are green and dark,
And have a brown and rough bark.

And when the leaves float to the ground,
They land down softly without a sound.
Who has seen more than those wonderful trees?
They've seen it all, even birds and bees.
The trees are a wonderful thing,
And from the top of them, in the summer, you
Hear the birds sing!

Debbie Millar (13)
Ballymena Academy

Pie

Apple pie, oh how I love it
I could eat five whole apple pies
And I probably wouldn't even be satisfied
Because it tastes so good, my stomach keeps growing.

Rhubarb pie, oh how I love it.
Its fruity mixture
And its rough texture,
Put together they make a lethal but tasty combination.

Shepherd's pie, oh how I hate it,
It has potatoes and mince,
But no outer crust.
What kind of pie has no crust?

Mince pie, oh how I hate it.
The outer crust is good and tasty
But as you dig deeper, what you look for isn't even there,
Why, oh why, isn't there any mince in a mince pie?

Pumulo Banda (13)
Ballymena Academy

Scars Of Bullying

The scars we have, some old, some new,
Some people have many, some people have few.
The ones from bullying don't go away,
They're in your heart and there to stay.

Tears are the words the heart can't say,
They got there by pain I endured today.
It was physical and verbal, both just as bad,
It makes your heart ache and tears you apart.

Don't suffer in silence, don't suffer at all,
Don't be afraid to say you'd pain in your heart today.
Tell someone you know, tell someone you trust,
So you can look forward to a brighter, painless day.

Lynsey Agnew (13)
Ballymena Academy

Fallen Angels

The rebel angels fell,
Garlanded with fire
Fell from Heaven's gate
For their hearts desire.

And in their descent, they screamed in anguish,
For their wings were set alight.
A blazing trail of angels,
Showered onto Earth
By the wrath of God.

And as the last angel fell,
He glimpsed what he was to be denied for eternity.
The Heavens closed upon him
And with that so did the glimmer of the Divine One vanish.

Denied paradise for eternity,
To be like men on Earth
Not angels anymore but,
Mortals doused in sorrow.

Now the angels feel pain,
Remorse and hatred,
They dwell among us
Igniting wars.

The angels find solace in despair,
Happiness in hate and joy in torment.
They feel not contentedness, nor death
But burden others of their mishap.

They live, breathe and die,
And are reborn again,
They are immortal
And so goes on the endless torment of knowing Hell

After all, what is Hell but the eternal absence of God?

Jennifer Jackson (15)
Ballymena Academy

Dreams

What I used to dream
Is now all so real
Something I can see
Something I can touch
Something I can feel.

Not all dreams
End with gladness
Some end with sorrow
Some end with despair
Some end with sadness

But not all is lost
In the journey of time
All I have ever wanted
All I have ever desired
All is now mine

This great dream
That takes me from reality
Ends with the fear
Ends with the darkness
Ends with calamity

But the truth hits me
Like a pain encrusted stone
Left in the cold
Left in the rain
Left all alone

What I had is gone
Truth makes its intrusion
Leaves me afraid
Leaves me alone
Leaves me away from my sweet illusion.

Lewis Edwards (13)
Ballymena Academy

Snow

It falls so lightly to the ground,
It doesn't even make a sound.
Gently it lands on the window sill,
Piling high it all sits still.

It falls from the trees,
Shaking in the breeze.
It lies so neat,
Crunching beneath your feet.

Children sledging on the hill,
The snowman standing very still.
His carrot nose and colourful hat,
He looks ever so jolly, round and fat.

Out pops the winter sun,
Spoiling all the children's fun.
All the snow it melts away,
What a pity it has to be that way.

Emma Davison (13)
Ballymena Academy

My New Kitten

My new kitten is a pest
I just got it the other day
The older cat behaves the best
The wee one only wants to play.

The kitten thinks it rules the house
It struts about and stuffs its face
It still can't even catch a mouse
But tried to throttle my shoelace.

The older cat is very wise
The kitten it must tolerate
And do its best not to despise
This little ball that's come of late.

Henry Patterson (12)
Ballymena Academy

Hallowe'en

Children tilting their heads up high,
To watch the fireworks in the sky,
Trick or treaters all around,
Making scary, ghostly sounds.

Pumpkins lit upon the ground,
While Catherine wheels whizz all around.
Fireworks are opening like buds,
And fizzing about like soapy suds.

Children are carrying bags of sweets,
While others are counting up their sweets,
Skeletons, witches, ghosts galore,
Knocking at the neighbour's door.

Hallowe'en can be a mystical time,
With scary stories and ghostly rhymes,
I hope you have a brilliant night,
And don't give yourself a scary fright.

Rebecca Huston (13)
Ballymena Academy

My Cat

He lies beside the fire,
All curled up in a ball,
He lies beside the fire,
In winter and in fall.

He is a tabby pussycat,
Like on the Whiskas ad,
Everybody loves him,
Me, my mum and dad.

Late at night when I'm in bed,
He jumps up like a flash,
He then curls up quite cosily,
Beside me and my ted.

Christine Maybin (12)
Ballymena Academy

The City

A wooden hovel in the trees,
A little man standing in the breeze.
Joined by another hut, then by four,
Soon a church and three homes more.
The tiny people ebb and flow,
As up the manors and markets grow.
Roads shoot out and wind away,
Carts come and go every day.
As they move they start changing
And soon the horse becomes an engine.
The dirt erupts with gleaming towers
And highways for their motor cars.
It blasts its way up through the sky,
To sparkle and shine way up high.
It burns its way across the land,
Bursting through mud and rock and sand.
It does not stop at the water's edge,
But forms itself into a ledge.
To race across the oceans deep,
Concealing it under the iron keep.
The lights flare up to blind the sun,
The planet enveloped, but not just one.
The arks of glass and silicon fly
And to the Earth they wave goodbye.
They float on through the heavens great,
Lying like an unspoilt slate.
The workers work to build and build,
Until the stars are all but filled.
From Earth until eternity,
There's no end to the great city.

Robert Martin (13)
Ballymena Academy

Characteristics Of My Cat

Her fur is the colour of wheat,
Except for her paws which are as white as sleet,
And her nose has black spots but is mainly brown,
She acts like royalty and should be wearing a crown.

When I lie down on the settee,
She curls up into a ball upon my knee,
I sometimes think she has a built in radar,
Cos when I come home from school she
Seems to sense it from afar.

Her eyes are a never ending hole,
They are her window to the soul,
She brings Christmas early by leaving
Presents at our door.

The longer she is with us,
I will love her more and more.

Andrew Carson (13)
Ballymena Academy

Music

Music comes in different types
There's classical, rock, pop, rap,
Heavy metal, dance, garage and tap.

Music comes in different genres,
Record stores have different stock,
But my favourite would have to be rock.

Nowadays you can carry music with you,
With all new technology
And you can tell how old the song is by chronology.

Everyone has their favourite song,
Young or old,
All music should be *bold!*

Karl Smith (13)
Ballymena Academy

Victory

Bang! is the signal, the race has begun
I lurch forward quickly and begin to run.
I'm at the very back now, of a never-ending line
But slowly, I make my way forward, one place at a time.
The race has been set in a beautiful place
I see and smell wild flowers as a cool breeze hits my face.
My stamina keeps me going, as I start to tire out
My concentration tripping, until I hear my mum shout,
'Run Charlene! Nearly there! Almost at the end!'
I catch sight of my coach as he screams,
'Sprint! The finish line's just up ahead!'
With my heart pounding in my chest, I quicken up my pace
All I can think of is winning, I won't settle for second place.
I start to feel quite dizzy
As blood pounds through my veins
Just one more person to overtake
Can I do it with all these pains?
I'm nearly right beside her now, we're almost neck and neck
When I hear a familiar voice shout,
'Get a move on, for goodness sake!'
I look up at the finish line, to see my older brother
Whose jumping excitedly up and down,
As I run through the finish line,
Into the arms of my proud mother.
'Congratulations!' the organiser says, whilst patting me on the back
'To Charlene Law for winning the race.'
As he lifts a large trophy off the rack.

Charlene Law (14)
Ballymena Academy

Inside A Boy's Head

Oh no! It's problem sums in maths again -
The teacher's calling out my name!
I haven't heard a word she said
With all the daydreams in my head.

It's really time that we were fed -
For lunch we're having soup and bread
Instead of satisfying our greed
The money will go to those in need.

Just one more class and then we're through
But I've loads of homework to do.
In school the learning hurts my brain
At home I do it all again!

Would you tell me, would you ever?
Why was I not born more clever?
Who was the guy who made the rule
That boys and girls must go to school?

Michael Blackwell (12)
Ballymena Academy

Summer

Summer is absolutely great,
There's nothing you could possibly hate!
The sun shines all day
So everyone can play.

You can stay up late at night,
Because there's no homework in sight!
You can go to Spain,
Where there's no rain.

Oh, isn't summer great?

Always remember summer's a blast,
So make the most of it, as it passes so fast!
If only, if only it could last!

Victoria Ross (13)
Ballymena Academy

The Hockey Player

'3-2-1' she said under her breath
The whistle went off
The centre forward passed her the ball
She passed it on and made a run up the pitch.

She was passed the ball again
But this time she saw a big open space,
She could either pass the ball or run
She made a decision and ran.

She ran with all her might
But she could feel the other team
Closing in on her,
She made a final effort and ran even harder.

She got into the circle
She brought her stick up and . . .
Bam!
She hit the ball into the back of the net.

The team cheered
Patting her on the back,
And shouting, 'Well done!'
She was happy!

Lois Wilson (12)
Ballymena Academy

Rebel

The machine has gone too far
We'll grab a rifle and a crowbar
It is time to liberate
And destroy the machine which we hate
We let out a battle cry
We'll fight this war until we die
They call us insubordinate
But we will fight, be sure of that
So rebel yell my brothers and
Let's liberate our people again.

Calum Allen (13)
Ballymena Academy

I Wish

I wish I was a grizzly bear,
Big and brown with fluffy hair.
My favourite thing is to roar,
But as well as that to sleep and snore.

I wish I was a butterfly,
Flap my wings and go up high.
In the daytime it's lovely and bright,
But at night it's such a beautiful sight.

I wish I was a scaly fish,
But never be served on a dish.
My favourite thing is to swim,
But if I meet an enemy, I will lose a limb.

I wish I was a shining star,
Though I couldn't drive a car.
From way down there I must look small,
But best of all I could give light to you all.

Judith Hanna (12)
Ballymena Academy

Snowy

(In memory of Snowy)

One Christmas Day I ran down the stairs,
To see what Santa got me for Christmas.
My mum said that it was very special,
When I went down to see it was a little white puppy.
I called him Snowy.
Over the years we grew real close,
I taught him to sit, stay and play.
When I was down he made me happy,
Till one day he lay dead in the corner,
Now no one makes me happy, I am sad and lonely.

Debbie Erwin (13)
Ballymena Academy

Mondays!

Mondays, Mondays, boring old Mondays,
It is the fact that I have to get up,
When I get disturbed from my slumber,
I find myself prone to lumber,
What is going to happen next?

I get ready for school thinking, *have I done my homework?*
My mum drives me to the front door and sends me off with goodbye.
All the kicking and screaming that awaits me ahead,
Sure will put a shock in the system.

First period Latin, and second, maths
And break only lasts for a few minutes.
By the time I pack my bag, it's off again to geography and English.
Lunch isn't so bad but the noise of the dinner hall I am used to.
Then pack my bags for home economics, at least it is just around
the corner.

When I come from cookery, now wide awake,
I am sure to get hit or to fall,
This is because hockey or netball awaits me.

Ah, home time at last, I know as my dog greets me and my dad
watches telly,
And then stuck into the homework,
When I have my dinner it is back out the door again
To see my sweetie-pie Belle.

No, she is not a friend, but an animal, yes,
A horse actually as it comes,
When I am done with her,
It is home to bed,
Ah, that's me done for another day!

Jodie-Lee Gordon (13)
Ballymena Academy

Christmas Time

Christmas is a special time of year
You just want to shout and cheer.

With snow falling on the ground
And children playing all around.

Snowmen dotted here and there,
I just want to stop and stare.

The shops are full of Christmas cheer,
With songs ringing out for all to hear.

Christmas lights they shine so bright,
Like the moon and stars in the sky at night.

Santa flying overhead,
While all the children are in bed.

All the children must be nice,
'Cause if they're not, they'll pay the price.

Chloe Kernohan (11)
Ballymena Academy

My Favourite Football Team

L is for Linfield football club
I is for incredible goals that they score
N is for noise of the crowd when the ball hits the back of the net
F is for football pitch that they play on
I is for incredible players
E is for excellent skill
L is for the love for the players when they score
D is for dream goals that they score

F is for the floodlights
C is for courage for taking on other teams.

Scott Lyle (12)
Ballymena Academy

Spring

This elegant lady sweeps the land
But no one can see her, but they feel
Her warm breath on their cheek
And smell her sweet perfume.

At dawn she wakens up the land
And the dew upon the grass
Is really her tears of sadness
For she knows her reign won't last.

In time she will be overcome
For summer's at her tail
So treasure those peaceful months
From March to pleasant June.

She dances and sings like a lark
And joyfully she roams
And while she's here she spreads her cloak
O'er the land and it is spring.

Rachel Thompson (12)
Ballymena Academy

Liverpool FC

L is for the legendary play on the field
I is for the incredible teamwork produced
V is for the vital players in the team
E is for excellence during play
R is for the respect given to each player
P is for the precise movement and tactics on the field
O is for optimum, skill and effort
O is for the obstacles which occur on the pitch
L is for the loyalty and support from the fans

F is for fame of what they've achieved
C is for Cisse's skill and devotion.

William Kennedy (12)
Ballymena Academy

Nature

Nature is so wonderful
So bright and very colourful
It keeps its looks all year round
Like a shrub in the ground

See the squirrels in the autumn
Storing acorns for the winter
Now the leaves change their colours
Getting ready to be blown away

'Tis the season to be jolly
See the robin eat the holly
Winter is a wonderland
When the snow covers land

Snowdrops, crocuses, daffodils
All the splendour of springtime
See the lambs dancing in the fields
Once again it's lambing time

Grass is cut
Flowers are growing
Yes you've guessed
It's summertime.

Nature is a gift from God
Given freely for us all
Spring, summer, autumn, winter
Nature never goes to sleep.

Matthew Mairs (11)
Ballymena Academy

Somewhere

She sits and rocks in silence,
Her chair goes back and forth,
Her hands clasped as if in prayer,
Her eyes look towards the empty chair.

Her hair is pinned up neatly,
As white as driven snow,
Her bony fingers tremble,
As she studies the rug below.

She gazes at the photos,
The silent tears they flow,
She still can't believe it,
The years they have gone so.

She smiles as she remembers,
How happy they used to be,
Their wedding day was wonderful,
The way it should always be.

But the war it came so quickly,
He was sent off to France,
The dreaded news arrived swiftly,
'He didn't stand a chance.'

Her days are almost over,
And with them her despair,
She always truly loved him,
They will meet again . . . somewhere.

Maeve Doyle (12)
Ballymena Academy

The Creepy Crawler

The creepy crawler is short and fat,
It has six eyes and a stomach that
Regurgitates each time it eats,
Its stomach does not agree with meat.

It scuttles and slithers across the ground,
Silently, without a sound,
It leaps and pounces for its prey,
Swallows it up and crawls away.

It lives under beds of girls and boys,
Instead of meat it feeds on toys.
The teddy bears you thought had gone missing,
Are inside the crawler's stomach, glistening.

So if you see this horrific sight,
Watch out for the creepy crawler's bite.
Before a minute you'll be dead,
Without another whisper said.

Niall McGowan (12)
Ballymena Academy

The Murcielago

The Murcielago is an amazing machine,
0 to 60 in 4.3
Big wide wheels and scissor doors,
This is a car that can't be ignored.

580 horsepower at your feet,
To own this car would be really neat,
Gleaming paint and body curves,
Driving this machine would take some nerve.

White leather interior and silver clocks,
This car is certainly not any old crock,
But alas all I can do is dream,
As my poster is the only one I've ever seen.

Thomas Moore (12)
Ballymena Academy

Mr C

My friend, Mr C,
Always copies me.
It can be annoying,
But sometimes flattering.

You see, Mr C knows,
What I wear, so
He puts on the same,
To reflect me is his aim.

When I am blue, he is as well.
But I am not sad, I feel
Clear and happy. Grey is being depressed
That is how he too is dressed.

We both look stunning.
At the end of the day, my son, running
Past to bed, leaves streaks of gold
Behind. He is very bold!

Rachel Cubitt (17)
Ballymena Academy

Pirates

One dark, foggy night
A pirate ship drifted ashore,
The man in the lighthouse did sight
This ship full of jewels galore.

The captain of the ship was well known
His name was Cruel Short John Gold,
Any disobedient sailors were thrown
Into the ocean cold.

They captured one of another crew
And made him walk the plank,
But when came the morning dew
The pirate ship sank!

Richard McNeill (11)
Ballymena Academy

School Rules!

A whisper here, a whisper there
A whisper everywhere,
The teacher's snoozing,
The girls' team is losing,
How did they get water bombs?

Chaos here, chaos there
Chaos everywhere,
The room's a mess
I've got a wet vest,
What's next?

Sacks here, sacks there
Sacks everywhere,
Stink bomb packs in the sacks,
Demolition and destruction
This room needs new construction,
Please wake up teacher.

Mess here, mess there
Mess everywhere,
The worst is I need some cars
I'm going to drive to Mars,
Dust, dirt and water now
How can this go on? How?

The headmaster's here.

Mark Herbison (12)
Ballymena Academy

My Dog

She runs as fast as a bolt of lightning
Through the trees, it must be frightening
In the stream she gets a drink
I often wonder why she doesn't sink.

In the garden on a summer's day
She always wants me to come and play
She loves to go and fetch her ball
But will return at my first call.

When it comes to bathtime, she will hide
Because she thinks it spoils her pride
After bath time she likes to roll
In a very, very muddy hole.

Down the road she goes for a walk
She also hears people talk
When I go she gives a frown
Then she goes and lies down.

Peter Knowles (11)
Ballymena Academy

Anything

Anything can be anything you want it to be,
It can be small, tall, deep, wide,
Round, straight, in or outside,
You can like it or hate it, smell it or taste it,
It's what you want it to be.

It can be over or under, lightning or thunder,
It can be yeah! very good, or no! what a blunder!
It can be your best friend or your arch enemy,
It's *anything* you want it to be!

Jake Wallace (11)
Ballymena Academy

The Writer Of This Poem

(Based on 'The Writer of this Poem' by Roger McGough)

The writer of this poem,
Is as strong as an ox,
As happy as a king,
As swift as a fox.

As wise as an owl,
As bold as brass,
As hungry as a wolf,
As brittle as glass.

As sturdy as an oak,
As steady as a rock,
As swift as a hawk,
As crafty as a fox.

The writer of this poem,
Never ceases to amaze.
He's one in a million,
(or so the poet says!)

Jordan McCullough (11)
Ballymena Academy

Last Day Of School

On the last day of school,
There is not one rule,
Things get broken,
From people joking,
Pranks are played,
No more fees to be paid,
With minutes to spare,
Then with a boom,
That must be the bell,
Then everyone charges out of the room!

Connor Worthington (11)
Ballymena Academy

Food And I

Chips, chips glorious chips,
No one dislikes a really good chip.
Golden brown, cooked to perfection,
Smothered in vinegar, ketchup on the side,
The only bad bit is realising you're finished.

Vegetables are great cooked in a pan,
With 0% fat they're everyone's faves,
Mixed in a blow, rice on the side,
Cooked in an oven, gas mark 5,
And then there you have it, the perfect main meal.

Chocolate o chocolate, where art thou?
I want to eat and swallow you now,
Tasty and delicious and come in different kinds,
Put it in a cake or melt it down,
For it is great in mint choc chip form.

As for breakfast, don't get me started,
From toast to cereals to fry-ups,
From footballers or models or you and me,
We all eat this meal of the day,
You know what; I'll have it right now.

Nathan Orr (13)
Ballymena Academy

Crystal

I have a special Crystal
It stays in a bowl on my shelf
I sometimes take it down
And gaze at it by myself

My Crystal isn't big
Its size is rather smallish
I love my Crystal lots
But Crystal is my pet goldfish!

Sara Bestek (11)
Ballymena Academy

The Frog

There it is,
still and green,
quiet and small,
wet and free.

Then suddenly,
it leaps off its spot,
onto dry land,
and sits with no movement.

Once more,
it springs from the ground,
except twice this time,
fearing the object behind.

It sits cautiously,
moving its eyes,
to catch sight of,
its foe.

All I wanted to do,
was touch this little,
amazing creature,
the frog.

Rachel Montgomery (12)
Ballymena Academy

Hide-Bound

Wings of words
Flying higher,
Spreading wide
The empty shells
Of long ago.

Letting go from up on high
Raging fire and cursed victor
Screech and roar
Grudges blazing.

Mutiny, brawl and
Eerie silence
As down they fall,
Like noble steeds
Of dragon hide.

Muted landing,
Hiding glances
Malevolent lies
A wing to it.

For, what have you done
You fearful beasts
Of modern times?

Rachel Swann (15)
Ballymena Academy

Seasons

On a pleasant spring morning
The birds freckle the sky
The flowers burst with love
On a joyful spring morning.

On a humid summer's day
The ocean of green grass flourishes
The sun melts on my skin
As the warm air surrounds me
On a joyful summer's day.

On a crunchy autumn evening
The bare, towering trees sway,
The crackling coloured leaves blanket the ground
As the ripe air surrounds me
On a joyful autumn evening.

On a starry winter night
The snow falls silently
The frost tickles rapidly
As the crisp air surrounds me
On a joyful winter's night.

Jessica Todd (11)
Ballymena Academy

My Sister

My sister is a fast ticking clock,
She is a pleasant day of May,
She is a bird because she swoops up high,
Her weather is rather sunny.

She is a washing machine because she never stops moving,
Her time is ten o'clock.
She is like a daffodil because she's always bright and happy,
She is as tall as a skyscraper.

Lauren McNair (11)
Ballymena Academy

Spring

The grass is wet with dew,
Trees standing straight and tall,
Never-ending branches surround
Me like a wall.

If you ever wonder,
Where I might be,
You'll find me on a summer seat,
With no one else beside me.

Please don't disturb me,
It's the only peace I get,
Safe in this heaven on Earth,
You'll be the first person I've met.

Why don't you find a place
Where dew freely falls,
Where no man does disturb
Only a cat on a wall?

Jessica Wilson (12)
Ballymena Academy

My Best Friend

He is like a rocking chair,
Always springing about.
A jolly, green clover,
A smart car, all complicated,
Like food because I like being round both,
Hard to play, like Twister,
Like a big hunk of wood, very thick,
A black sheep who sometimes strays away.

Jonathan McGaughey (11)
Ballymena Academy

The Match

I am queuing outside for my ticket,
Gazing at the stadium in front.
Finally now, the queue is moving,
As we watch our opponents taunt.

Now I have got my ticket,
And the people are flocking in,
Through the red and white electric doors,
Then we all begin to sing.

Inside the stadium is a great place to be,
Although the opposing fans were abrupt.
Now here come the home team,
Get ready, the stadium is about to erupt!

What a game I saw take place,
Nothing like ever before.
The end result was three-nil to us,
But to me it was so much more.

The intricate passing,
The one touch play,
The silky skills,
All to the opponents' dismay.

It was the best game of the season I reckon,
It was just so much fun.
Pity that's the season over,
But bring on the next one!

James Loughridge (12)
Ballymena Academy

My Family

We're like the four musketeers,
My sister is a number one girl,
You wouldn't give her away for the world,
She's like a mouse in the house,
Her hair's as fair as a blonde bear,
She would give you a scare,
She's as small as a telephone call,
And as rowdy as a fight in the hall.

My mum, she's as nice as curry and rice,
She's as fit as a fiddle,
She's the best cook in the world,
She makes Jamie Oliver look like a mouse.

My dad, he's definitely rad,
He's totally mad,
He's as tall as a tree
And still bigger than me when standing on the settee,
But that's Dad for you.

This is what we're like,
That's all from me, Spike.

Luke McMullan (11)
Ballymena Academy

My Mum

She's a warm jumper made from the finest wool.
She's a daisy with perfectly shaped petals and a lovely scent.
She's a strawberry cream chocolate with a white chocolate swirl.
She's a cuddly, soft teddy bear with round, furry paws.
She's the month of August bringing us all hopes of joy.
She's a moist cake with chocolate icing on top.
She's the sound of birds tweeting on a bright summer's morning
And she's a fluffy pillow made from soft Mongolian fur!

Marianne Stoker (11)
Ballymena Academy

Bittersweet

Along the beach we flew as one,
Wrapped up in our own song.
Creating our own harmonies,
But the rhythm then went wrong.

He slowly sank beside the sea
His heart was fading fast.
His eyes grew dim, I called to him,
My Rocky breathed his last.

I saw the imprint on the sand
Where my sweet Rocky lay,
I felt his warm breath on my hand
Yet he had gone away.

I turned around and saw my pony,
His ghost above the sea.
I realised now my special friend
Had come back to comfort me.

Now the dream is over
The imprint washed away,
My Rocky came to say goodbye
And in my heart he'll stay.

Lizzy Graham (13)
Ballymena Academy

Christmas

C hristmas is a special time of year
H opeful to see some red-nosed reindeer
R ound the town everybody's jolly
I vy and holly inside the house
S now falling gently like a mouse
T rees lit up all bright
M ary and Joseph in the stable at night
A ll the hustle and bustle of children's play
S anta is on his way.

Stephen Shaw (11)
Ballymena Academy

Badger

He walks around the woodland floor
Collecting food to fill his store.
He has to fill it for a reason,
So he has enough for the winter season.
Then he crawls into his little bed
And waits until it's spring again.

So when he sleeps, he dreams about
What happens when he goes back out.
He dreams about the gleaming light,
The sun is shining strong and bright.
He ponders about his animal friends
And what they are doing in their little dens.

When spring comes, he goes outside
And looks around with joy and pride.
He meets his friends and they all embrace,
They're glad to see each other's face.
Another year has passed, we're in his den
And he's out collecting food again.

Jordan Foster (11)
Ballymena Academy

Racing Cars

R aring to go
A ccelerating away from the start, trying to take the lead
C hanging direction, trying to pass
 I nto a corner, braking hard
N ever losing concentration
G uiding the car through the course

'C an I win?' they ask themselves
A m I fast enough?
R ound the final bend
S uccess at the end.

Michael Caithness (12)
Ballymena Academy

Hallowe'en

Hallowe'en is coming soon,
With hopefully a full moon,
Fireworks crackling through the air,
How I love to stand and stare.

Fiery colours will abound,
Along with many different sounds,
Ghouls and ghosties everywhere,
Oh, what costume should I wear?

Children off to trick or treat,
How many vampires will they meet?
Off to the bonfire, a spectacular show,
Hear it crackle, watch it glow.

Walking home alongside the ditch,
I just hope I don't meet a witch,
The thought of home and warm apple pie,
What was that shape that just fluttered by?

Why, silly me, sure it was only a bat,
But I keep running and trip on a cat.
There's a light in the hall, someone's at home,
Very soon I'll be safely tucked up in my room.

Peter Clark (11)
Ballymena Academy

The Eagle

He clasps the crag with crooked hands
Close to the sun in lonely lands
Ringed with the azure world, he stands

The wrinkled rat runs for his life
The eagle's eyes are like searchlights
Looking everywhere for his prey

And when the eagle catches his prey
He is as proud as an elephant and his trunk.

Matthew Corbett (12)
Ballymena Academy

Homeless

He lies in the doorway,
Not a sound does he make.
He's dirty and unshaven,
His clothes all dishevelled.
With eyes that are sad and lonely,
Hands blackened and cut,
He's missing a shoe
And there's a hole in his sock.

People walk past him
Along the busy street,
While some sneak a glance,
Others his eyes can't meet.
They don't have a care,
Or a worry in the world,
While the old man lies there,
Lonely and unnoticed.

Cherith O'Hara (12)
Ballymena Academy

My Cat, Meg

Meg is the only cat for me,
She is cute and cuddly,
But if you are a small animal,
A rabbit, mouse, bird or vole,
Her killer instincts will take their toll.

Spring is the best time to be a hunter,
When the animals are smallest,
But she stays inside in the winter
And finds where it is warmest.

They say black cats are unlucky,
Meg is almost totally black,
But I find that she is lucky,
Lucky enough to have a loving family,
Lucky enough to be with me.

Connor Fleming (11)
Ballymena Academy

My Holiday

Down at the beach one summer's day,
I see waves crash and palm trees sway.
People talking, eating, laughing,
Children running, jumping, splashing.
Umbrellas up and towels down,
The beach is as crowded as a Saturday in the town.

But then I feel a drip on my shoulder,
Look up at the sky and feel a bit colder.
The rain was coming pelting down,
A storm had risen and I could do nothing but frown.

People grabbing, running, shivering,
Children shouting, screaming, quivering.
Drenched from my head to my toes,
I just stood there and froze.

So much for my day at the beach!

Jessica Nevin (11)
Ballymena Academy

My Cat, Lucky

He waits outside in the garden,
Looking for a mouse,
And if he ever catches one,
It's certain he won't be allowed in the house.

But if the poor mouse struggles,
Or tries to get free,
There is no chance for the little mouse
And on the mat there will be a present for me!

Lucky is left alone outside,
And he will start to cry,
As he wants to sneak inside,
If the door is ever opened, it's certain he will try!

Sarah Lowery (11)
Ballymena Academy

Christmas!

The time of year that is covered with snow,
When sleet falls and cold winds blow,
Even though it's cold and wet,
Christmas is still my favourite time of year,
It's full of fun, laughter and cheer.
Putting up the Christmas tree is always really fun,
There are cards and letters in the post almost every day,
Lots of enjoyable games to play,
Decorations in the hall, snowmen, carols, I love it all!
Another thing that I really enjoy,
Filling a shoe box full of gifts and toys,
For a little child far away,
I hope that it will make their day.

Christmas wishes from family and friends,
I wish that Christmas would never end!
Then there's the excitement of Christmas Eve,
Movies and music,
Also, of course, Santa comes, then leaves.
Jack Frost also generally pays a visit,
Some people say what he leaves is a touch of magic,
Sometimes I wonder . . . really? Is it?

Ruth Gracey (11)
Ballymena Academy

A Starry Night

As I looked out the window one starry night,
Fireworks went off to my delight.
I sat and watched all night long,
Humming the tune of my favourite theme song.
The wind howled, the trees rustled,
And something rattled in the shed.
A dog howled, a cat miaowed,
It frightened me to death.
I couldn't stay up anymore!
So I lay down and slept in my bed.

Victoria Marcus (11)
Ballymena Academy

The Scrambler Race

I'm in the pits,
Scared out of my wits,
I'm ready to go,
Though I'll never win.

I'm at the start,
Ready to go,
But I hope not slow,
The gate goes down, off I go!

I get a good start,
Off like a dart,
A guy is up my rear,
And I'm shaking with fear.

I'm near the end,
Racing against my friend,
I go over the line
And that's the scrambler race!

Stefan Kerr (11)
Ballymena Academy

A Poem

I was asked to write a poem,
About anything.
An Indian elephant,
Or a miserable king.

The Amazon rainforest,
The ancient Greeks,
Computer technology,
Of whizz-kid freaks.

A strong, graceful swan,
The most loyal friend,
I could go on forever,
But here I must end.

Roshni Janarthanan (13)
Ballymena Academy

Hallowe'en

Hallowe'en, Hallowe'en,
Best time of the year.
Hallowe'en, Hallowe'en,
Ghosts and ghouls appear.
Hallowe'en, Hallowe'en,
We go trick or treating.
Hallowe'en, Hallowe'en,
We come back half sleeping.
Hallowe'en, Hallowe'en,
Fireworks exploding in the sky.
Hallowe'en, Hallowe'en,
Nuts and apple pie.
Hallowe'en, Hallowe'en,
Sparklers that shine.
Hallowe'en, Hallowe'en,
What a colourful time.

Ian Wilson (11)
Ballymena Academy

Lost Puppy

I sat on a step,
Feeling lost and alone,
I desperately feared,
He'd never come home.
He'd run away quickly,
Leaving marks on the ground,
But try as I might,
He was nowhere to be found.
His little fluffy coat,
I longed to cuddle,
When I took him on my knee,
I didn't mind if he left a puddle.
The thought of him never being there,
Was one thought I couldn't bear.

Bronagh Gallagher (14)
Ballymena Academy

Homework

Why do we get homework?
We work enough through the day,
Concentrating and thinking hard,
Too much work . . . no play.
Then just before the bell rings,
The teacher shouts out loud,
'Get your homework books out.'
She points to the exercise and says,
'This is for tomorrow.'
Everyone groans and says,
'We've already got loads.'
Just as you finish copying it down,
Ding! The bell goes.
You pack up and evacuate the room,
Only once you're out you realise, *no,*
Another eight periods to go!
It's gonna be a long day.

George Hargy (12)
Ballymena Academy

My Dog

I have a dog called Borris who isn't very tall,
He loves it when I play with him
And he's good at catching the ball.
We taught our dog to sit quite some time ago,
I'd like to teach him other tricks
But he just doesn't seem to know.
Borris loves it when he sees his lead,
He knows he's getting a walk,
He's quite a clever little dog
And it would be great if he could talk.
Sometimes he can be bad
And sometimes he can be good,
But his most favourite pastime
Is food, food, food!

Jonathan Best (12)
Ballymena Academy

The Race

The engines are revving,
The lights are changing,
They will soon be off
And some will be raging,
For around the first corner someone will spin,
That might determine who will win.

The rain is falling on the track,
The tyres are screeching,
Like bats in attack.
As they come round the corner,
The spectators gasp,
As one of the drivers spins onto the grass.

In the pit stop the mechanics are tense,
They can hear the cars whizzing past the pit's fence.
As the end draws near,
The marshals raise the flag,
The crowds all cheer as the winner knows he has the race in the bag.

Joel McNeilly (12)
Ballymena Academy

My Mum

She is like a beautiful pink rose
So gentle, yet very thorny
She's like a tiger with her foes
And can be very angry and stormy.

She's like a big, strong table
She is like a strong cup of coffee
And keeps us all very stable
Gorgeous and sticky and lovely as toffee.

She is like a big duvet
So warm and cuddly in the night
She is like a funny movie
So funny and smart and bright.

Sam McDowell (11)
Ballymena Academy

The Chestnut Tree

Every year I sit and wait,
Hoping that it could be autumn again,
I sit alone stuck in the ground,
Nobody here, nobody around.

I wish, I wish that somebody would notice me,
Then come and plant more trees next to me,
But it's hopeless when I'm stuck in here,
Away from sight,
So nobody can see my sad and lonely face.

Spring came and so did summer,
And autumn has come,
It's here again,
I hear the children run and shout,
They're coming, they're coming into sight.

They reach where I stand,
Take one look and run away,
Why, oh why can't I be like them,
All surrounded by children chooring and having fun?

Time passed ever so slowly that day
As I watched the children play,
And still I sit,
With nothing to say,
Waiting for my turn,
My turn to have fun,
But all I can do is wish for that day.

Claire Gillen (12)
Ballymena Academy

My Dream Machine

Four years, ten months, seven days,
The countdown is on . . .
Till I reach the important date, *when?*
It's the third of August, 2010.

You ask me why this date is important,
Surely it's just another day!
But for me it's my 17th birthday,
I'm gonna get my licence
And drive my car away!

Like every boy, it's my dream to drive,
Attracting the ladies to my car's side.
I wanna Porsche Carrera or a Range Rover,
Something very sporty and fast,
But I do want my car to last!

Samuel McNabney (12)
Ballymena Academy

Words

The sneering faces stare and laugh,
As the cruel, bitter poison is injected into her,
She tries to flee,
The brightly coloured displays mock her,
Running down the corridor, out through the door,
Tears flowing down her face,
The memories haunt her,
Is she really so despised?
Is there any cure for this pain?

No, there is no escape from the words,
Which aim to hurt and destroy lives.
Bruises will fade, cuts will heal,
But the sting and venom of words may last forever.

Rachel Ferguson (14)
Ballymena Academy

Pollution

A good, clean world,
Is what we need,
No more pollution,
Do a good deed.

Environment friendly,
Eco mad,
Lead-free petrol,
'Come on, Dad!'

Recycle bottles,
Recycle tin,
Recycle paper,
Put it in the recycling bin!

No more pollution,
No more litter,
A good environment,
Come on! Don't be bitter!

Nicole Connor (11)
Ballymena Academy

Running

When I run
I feel light as a cloud,
Free as a bird.
I don't look around me.
I think of nothing.
I just focus
On my pounding feet. Running.
My legs are strong.
They work tirelessly.
I challenge myself
To run faster and faster.
My mind is empty.
I just run and run.

Conor McKeown (12)
Ballymena Academy

Inside The Darkness

I lie awake at midnight
And listen to the clock strike twelve times.
Silence!
One car drives past my window.

The darkness closes in on me,
I just want to escape.
Silence!
I wish I was in a happier place.

The window frame rattles,
The thunder violently roars.
Silence!
But still the lightning flashes on.

The clock strikes one,
My eyes flicker closed.
Silence!
As the whole house sleeps.

Nicola Stewart (13)
Ballymena Academy

Moonlight Disco

Flowing, silky tops that glitter,
In the moonlight's glare,
Satin trousers, smooth and soft,
That show your underwear.

Strappy shoes with clicky heels,
Tap-tapping on the ground,
Scruffy trainers, wearing away,
So soft they make no sound.

Loud music blaring out,
Gives that happy feeling,
People dancing all around,
The stars and moon, their ceiling.

Jordan Tweedy (13)
Ballymena Academy

Go On, I Dare You!

Water is like thousands of diamonds shining in the light of the sun.
We use it for showers, washing up and water fights! So much fun!
But many, many people don't have much of it,
It is usually for them found in a muddy ditch.

Food, glorious food and for you it is really good,
We have it every day, breakfast, lunch and play,
But many, many people don't have much of it,
They don't even have enough to live.

These two things I have mentioned might seem rather odd,
Yes, we do have water and food, two peas in a pod.
But many, many people that live quite far away,
Haven't got much and alive they cannot stay.

It is a race against time.
You can give all your money to help them out of this grime,
But the best thing you can do, just to show you care,
Go on, I dare you just to say a short, simple prayer.

Abigail McCready (13)
Ballymena Academy

Will There Ever Be A Rainbow?

Will there ever be a rainbow,
So I can watch it glimmer
And observe how the colours flow,
As well as seeing them shimmer?

Never before have I set eyes on one,
I do not know why,
People think it is not fun,
But every day I gaze into the sky.

But on one rainy day,
I spot a rainbow in the sky,
And I think *oh my!*

Andrew Byers (13)
Ballymena Academy

My World

The world is spinning all around me
Until it stops and I see it -
I see the bright, glowing land.
Bright flowers and soft music
Send thoughts flowing through my mind.

I think I'm in Heaven.

Waterfalls glisten and sparkle and gleam
The rivers are smooth and inviting
The trees sway gently in the breeze.
All seems so peaceful, so quiet, so calm
This is my place, my world, my mind.

I think I'm in Heaven.

In my world there are no broken hearts
No sorrow or tears or anger
No fighting or war, no terror.
If only the real world were like this
But that is only a fantasy.
Instead,
All I can do is
Think that I'm in Heaven.

Emma McKay (13)
Ballymena Academy

My Friend, Thomas

My friend, Thomas
Is like a tiny carpet, all covered in fur and wool.
He is like a funny April fool on a cool April day.
Thomas is very get up and go, like an energetic Saturday.
He is like a laugh track, added onto a very funny TV show.
He is like a sweet sauce and good in big doses.
Thomas is like an aspirin who will cure all the blues!
He is like the donkey in Shrek, small and hilarious.
He is like the colour blue, calm and cool!

Jamie Brown (12)
Ballymena Academy

My New School

My new school is really cool
Beats the rest, it really rules
I get up early in the morning to catch the bus
I'm used to it now and it's no real fuss
Get to the station and walk up the path
Seeing the grounds that this school hath
Lots of new people from different places
And also familiar faces
Many new sports
And even tennis courts
Lots of new classes
The pupils come down the corridor in masses
In the cafeteria they serve delicious meals
They also throw in some great deals
In the science lab
It is really fab
In home economics you make great food
But only if you're good
In history
We solved a mystery
There's lots to remember - books, files and smart card
Remembering it all can be quite hard
But overall
My new school is really cool!

Adam McDowell (11)
Ballymena Academy

Home

A wet night:
I struggle to find my key,
My clothes are heavy with rain.
The street lights reflect in the puddles,
The cars swish through the flooded street.

My cold fingers search agonizingly
In my saturated pockets.
At last I locate the front door key
And stab repeatedly until it slides
Satisfyingly into the lock.

The front door opens
And the warm, cosy feeling caresses my tired body.
Someone has lit the fire:
The logs crackle in the grate.

The smell of cooking filters down the hall;
I hear a squeal of delight from the landing.
My small son stands already in his jammies,
His hair still wet from his warm bath.

My heart fills with pride and contentment -
I'm home.
A winter night in Ballymena.
Maybe it's not too bad after all!

Rachel Harkness (13)
Ballymena Academy

Bullying

I remember being bullied,
When I was at school.
Now, when I think about it,
I feel like a fool.

They'd push me and shove me
And they'd call me nasty names,
Though *they* were the fools,
Playing childish games.

I thought I was the only one,
They would pick upon,
But everywhere was full of victims,
Bullies would prey upon.

A note to all victims
Of bullying anywhere,
Don't keep things bottled up,
Tell a friend who'll care.

Shantelle French (13)
Ballymena Academy

Gran

She is an old, soft chair covered in cosy material.
She acts the way a bird acts about its chicks.
August is her month where it's sunny
And the gentle breeze sways the lovely tulips.
She is like chocolate as when you're sad
She can really cheer you up, in a nice way.

Shannon Cameron (11)
Ballymena Academy

An Invisible Force

The wind is invisible,
Not seen by man,
The effects are unmissable,
Hidden power across the land.

Leaves are pushed about,
By the cloudy breath,
Floating and swooping,
Till no leaves are left.

The wind can be a dangerous force,
Like the night's howling scream,
Destroying trees and buildings,
People's lives turned upside down,
Like a roller coaster dream.

Hurricanes and deadly tornadoes,
Rip the Earth apart,
In all things that blow about,
The invisible force plays a part.

Mark Johnston (13)
Ballymena Academy

My Friend

My friend is a boxer, with lots of spirit.
He is a footrest I can lean on.
He is a carrot because his hair is orange.
He is a cup, small and round.
He is a sneaker, he gets everywhere.
He's a great Man U supporter, he goes to every match.
Overall, he is like a footrest, someone you can rely on.

Richard French (11)
Ballymena Academy

Summer

It's the end of June,
School's almost out,
Happy days in the park,
Children laugh and shout.

Off on our hols,
Lazy days by the pool,
Having so much fun,
Don't think about school.

Happy evenings by the barbecue,
The smell of freshly cut grass,
Dad enjoys a beer or two,
From a long, cool glass.

Then all too soon summer comes to an end,
It's back to the grind,
But since I see all my friends again,
I really don't mind!

Sophie Coulter (14)
Ballymena Academy

My Brother

My brother is a battered old sunflower,
He's a noisy, loud electric guitar,
He is a scruffy, wet dog,
He's like sour, out of date milk,
My brother's a dull character,
But sometimes he can be a fun, sunny Saturday
Staying up to midnight.
He is like the month of December -
Fun, exciting and the month you want to get to.

Michael McMullan (11)
Ballymena Academy

Sailing

The sun has risen
And the day has begun,
The wind is strong,
But the sea is calm.

Go down to the harbour,
And rig up your boat,
Your troubles will soon be gone,
When you sail away.

You'll soon be flying,
Just you wait,
Gliding along the waves,
Carefree as a child.

When you step in that boat,
Joy will fill your heart,
When you step in that boat,
You can sail away to your heart's content.

Tom Foster (13)
Ballymena Academy

Baby

He is a young, new, cosy sofa,
Covered with silk.
He is a blow horn on a ship.
He has the head of a vulture.
He is a cuddly bear.
He has the mouth of a toothless grandpa.
He sometimes smells of your garbage can.
His fingers are made of runner beans.
His eyes are made of deep wells
And his ears are radar dishes.

Steven Young (11)
Ballymena Academy

The Weekend

It's last period on Friday,
The week is nearly over,
But . . . we're stuck in maths class.
15 minutes to go.

The teacher drones on, and on,
Doesn't she realise nobody's listening?
Everyone's urging the bell to ring.
10 minutes to go.

We're all thinking about the weekend,
Not square numbers,
And whether we're going to get homework or not.
5 minutes to go.

'Homework,' she barks.
'No,' we collectively groan.
'Oh alright, since it's the weekend, I'll let you off.'
'Yes, she has a heart after all!'
1 minute to go.

The bell rings,
A cheer goes up,
Two days of freedom,
Let's make the most of it!

Matthew Dick (13)
Ballymena Academy

All Around Me

On the watch tower
The night stretches endlessly before me
But I must stay awake
The enemy could be anywhere
I must stay awake . . .

The battle rages around me
Arrows fly around me
Swords clash around me
Shields smash around me

Blood gushes around me
Spears lay around me
People slain around me
Extreme pain around me

Fighting with my cloak
It is all a dream
But I am supposed to be on watch!
The enemy is prowling across the plain

I ring the warning bell
And I open the gates
The army rush out to meet the enemy
The battle rages around me . . .

Matthew Gaston (13)
Ballymena Academy

Hockey!

'Ground, stick,
Ground, stick,
Ground, stick -
Go!'
Yell the hockey players
As they trudge through the snow.

Shivers wriggle up their spines
As the wind howls in their ears.
The wild supporters, voices hoarse,
As they chant and scream their cheers.

Players stampede to the race,
As suddenly the ball from nowhere spins!
Supporters screaming, feet thumping,
The right wing shoots, scores and wins!

How great the feeling must have been,
When the referee's whistle shrilled!
A deep breath, a sigh, a cheer, a scream -
The winning team are thrilled.

Victoria McDowell (14)
Ballymena Academy

My Girlfriend

My girlfriend is hot like the month of July,
As nice to look at as an early sunset,
She is a light to light up my life,
She is as beautiful as a newborn kitten,
She is a holiday to look at,
She is as sweet as a pack of sweets,
She is as amazing as a new Ferrari car,
As lovely as a blooming rose,
A juicy apple hoping to be the one that I pick,
She is as exciting as a red and light purple sunset shining in the sky.

Ethan Archer (11)
Ballymena Academy

The Storm

A dreadful storm is blowing in,
The nice, hot sun can never win.
It starts to rain so I dash inside,
Where I can always hide.

I sit at the window and watch the sky,
The purple lightning lights up my eye.
The roar of the thunder gives me a fright,
Nothing could beat this legendary sight.

A big strike here and a big strike there,
To go outside would be a dare.
The reviews are in and this one's a beast,
Everyone likes lightning the least.

Clash and bang go the clouds up high,
Then, loudly, I let out a sigh.
Will it ever end? It's really bad,
And it's driving the dog mad!

Kyle Magee (13)
Ballymena Academy

My Sister

She is a cool, trendy leather sofa,
She is August because she loves the summer holidays,
She is like a thunderstorm when she gets mad,
She is a pair of jeans because she loves to be trendy,
She is Spain because she loves the hot weather,
My sister is a cool cat,
She is a really fast car like a Ferrari
Because when she chases me she goes really fast.
My sister is just my sister.

Claire Devlin (11)
Ballymena Academy

The Try

The referee blew the whistle,
The out-half kicked the ball high in the air.
The fat forwards run up in a line,
Like charging cavalry.
The ball is caught, passed
Out the backline.

The centre side steps.
He's through!
Tackled by the fullback.
'Ruck,' shouts the skipper.
'Push,' shout the props.
Ball won.
Offside!

Quick tap penalty.
He kicks the ball ahead.
No one calls.
Ballymena skipper
Catches it again.
Is he through?
Score!

Timothy McBride (14)
Ballymena Academy

The Somme

As the sun came up on that fateful day,
Eyes open wide,
In the muddy trenches where the soldiers lay,
Side by side,
Waiting for the command to make their way.

It came at last,
Forward they ran to meet their destiny,
Guns fired fast.
What happened next I cannot say,
Few survived the blast.

Steven Mairs (13)
Ballymena Academy

School

A buzzing sound in the classroom
Until the teacher charges in:
'Get out your books
And stop worrying about your looks!'

Our eyes surreptitiously on the clock,
We focus on its tick, tick, tock.
Will this lesson ever end?
I want to gossip with my friend.

Staring out the window,
I'm startled by a roar!
She demands of me an answer,
My eyes turn to the floor . . .

What is the answer?
My mind starts to race.
She edges still closer,
She's too 'in my face' . . .

All of a sudden -
Saved by the bell!
With glee I escape
From my school prison cell.

Esther McKane (13)
Ballymena Academy

Football

F antastic skill and control
O utstanding shooting and goal scoring abilities
O verall a brilliant game by the defenders
T he best fans the world has ever seen
B eastly decisions by the referee
A ccuracy in free kicks like you've never seen before
L uck like never before when the goalie saves a penalty
L osers are the other teams when we beat them at least 4-0.

Jonathan Watson (12)
Ballymena Academy

What Shall I Be Today?

As I wake up every day,
I ask myself the question,
What shall I be today?
Has anyone got a suggestion?

I could be angelic
And not do anything wrong,
But if I tried to be like this,
I wouldn't last very long.

I could be quite wicked
And obviously act really bad,
But if I tried to be like this,
I'd end up very sad.

I could be quite chatty,
I would spread the word,
But this would maybe take a while,
To make sure everyone heard.

I could be a lot of things,
The best of which would be,
Being someone I know best,
Being just like *me!*

Lauren Agnew (13)
Ballymena Academy

My Friend The Owl

A little surprise awaits
In the forest at night
Something with mystical eyes
Gleaming with delight.

It glides through the trees
As if lurking around
A swoop of its wings
Hunting, not making a sound.

Its accuracy is superb
Its hearing is keen
Its eyes are daring
Nothing can remain unseen.

The animal swoops
To catch its prey
Nothing can stop it now
Try though it may.

Gliding back to its young
Another night ends
I love these beautiful birds
The owls are my friends.

Fiona Magill (11)
Ballymena Academy

Playground Bully

I sat in the playground very still,
When my friend came and sat beside me,
Her name was Jill.
'What are you doing, my little mate?
Sitting here all alone, you could be late.'
Suddenly, I heard the fear of all my fears,
A deep rumbling going straight through my ears.
'Help! He's coming, the bully,' I cried
And through my little eyes I spied,
The massive bully with his leather coat on,
With his studded boots covered in frogspawn.
He was coming towards me, I was full of alarm,
I started to run, but he caught my arm.
He grabbed me by the scruff of the neck
And started to take everything
Out of my pockets and everywhere,
Till I stood there with nothing to spare.
Fortunately, the bell rang.
The bully then ran, not turning back,
Straight to the line.

I followed in despair!

Adam McIlmoyle (11)
Ballymena Academy

Beaches

B each balls bouncing up and down
E veryone having fun
A ll around you can see
C hildren smiling in the sea
H orses galloping on the sand
E verything is going just grand
S pectacular day out like we planned.

Tory Alexander (11)
Ballymena Academy

Irish Dancing

Tighten laces, buckle straps
Polish shoes, tights brand new
Every strand of hair perfectly in place
Walk on the stage, line of three
Fixed smile upon my face
One on each side and in the middle, me
Legs stretched, back straight
Feet at the ready, the music begins
We all want to win
Two and a half minutes will decide our fate
We all cross our feet and try to impress
Then the bell goes, we all stop dead
Walk to where we began and give a little bow
Not long until we know . . .
Who's the best dancer?

Anne Devlin (13)
Ballymena Academy

How To Write A Poem

When I try to write a poem
It's despair
At a blank
I sit and grimly stare
I'm so fed up
I've given up hope
So I'll go to my room
And quietly mope.

Wordsworth and Keats
Didn't have this trouble
But here I am with my head in a muddle
My sister, the student, says, 'Structure' and 'Time'
But between you and me she's a bit of a moan.

If this doesn't work, I'll be the class fool
And I'll be the laughing stock of the school.

Amy Finlay (13)
Dallymena Academy

The West End Show

Finally it was my time to shine and perform,
I had waited for this chance ever since I was born.
As soon as that last scene
Had died away,
I would storm onto the stage of the West End play.

As I ranted and raved
And plotted and crept,
The audience clapped, awed
And wept
At my amazing performance in the West End play
I think I should do this as a job every day!

When I took my final bows in front of the crowd
I heard the cheers clear and loud.
Then I smiled with the utmost glee
As a thought occurred that satisfied me -
There'll always be another play or scene
For me to shine and perform fantastically!

Michael Walker (12)
Ballymena Academy

My Mum

My mum can be as delicate as a rose or as hard as a thorn.
My mum is like a warm bed, soft and reassuring.
My mum can be as fast as a cheetah, yet is usually as slow as
a tortoise.
My mum is like a Saturday night, the best day of the week.
My mum is as soft as the touch of a feather.
My mum is like an old sofa, always glad when you see it.
My mum is like cool spring water after a hot day.
My mum is like a clown, bringing a smile to your face.
My mum is simply great.
Hope I get more pocket money, hee, hee!

David Anderson (11)
Ballymena Academy

Papa And Granny

Papa:
He is an old, comfortable sofa
And a soft, cute teddy bear.
He is beans on toast
With a steaming hot chocolate and marshmallows.
He is a Friday afternoon
Wrapped up in a fur coat
And a warm, cosy December evening
Sitting beside the fire.

Granny:
She is a soft, luxurious pillow
And a flower in bloom.
She is a warm summer night
With a gentle breeze in your hair.
She is a sleepy Sunday morning
With breakfast in bed
And a hot fudge sundae
With a creamy chocolate sauce.

Amy Hawthorne (11)
Ballymena Academy

The Eagle

Soaring in the sky,
Searching with my magnificent eye.

I hover above a field of wheat,
Looking for something that I could eat.

Any sudden movements, I'll be aware,
And then I'll swoop down, with the greatest of care.

The concentration is intense,
Having patience makes sense.

Because at the end of the day,
I'll get my prey.

Michaela Gallagher (14)
Ballymena Academy

That Word, 'Christmas'

When one mentions that word 'Christmas'
What images spring to mind?
Carol singers, Christmas puddings,
That awkward present to find.

When one mentions that word 'Christmas'
Is it that wonderful time of the year
When everyone is sending cards
And spreading festive cheer?

When one mentions that word 'Christmas'
Are all our thoughts so good?
Do we think of those poor souls
Suffering from lack of food?

When one mentions that word 'Christmas'
What does it really mean?
The birth of Jesus Christ
And the beautiful nativity scene.

When one mentions that word 'Christmas'
What will you think this year?
Getting together as a family,
That's the thought that I hold dear.

Jonathan Nevin (12)
Ballymena Academy

Death

It takes you by surprise,
It sneaks up on you when you least expect it,
It is as silent as a slithering snake
And as unpredictable as the weather.
It can strike at any time,
It is lurking in the shadows,
It can be anyone or anywhere,
Some people think it is peaceful,
But they would be wrong,
It is silent, but don't let that fool you . . .

Patrick Millar (11)
Ballymena Academy

A Winter's Night

There's nothing like a winter's night,
A cosy fire, you're wrapped up tight.
Some hot chocolate in a cup,
Nothing better to warm you up.

Just outside, softly falls the snow,
Leaving in its path a moonlit glow.
On the branch of a frosty birch,
A cheeky robin comes to take its perch.

The family gathers round the heat
Of a mesmerising fire of burning peat.
Brothers and sisters laugh and play,
There is no sadness, there's no dismay.

A hot water bottle heats the bed,
A place to rest your sleepy head.
There's nothing like a winter's night,
A cosy bed, you're wrapped up tight.

Hannah Martin (12)
Ballymena Academy

Poem

He is like a broken radio,
Lying in the dump.
He is like Thursday afternoon,
On an overcast day.
He is like late winter,
Cold and dark.
He makes a sound like a rhino,
Angry and mad.
He is like a Brussels sprout,
That was out of date last year.
He is like a wild cat,
Alert and dangerous.
He is like a bottle of lemonade,
Shaken with force.

Thomas O'Brien (11)
Ballymena Academy

Hallowe'en

Fireworks are noisy
Fireworks are loud
When they explode
They make a colourful cloud.

Kids call at neighbours' doors
'Trick or treat?' they say
Food or sweets they hope to get
On this special day.

A Hallowe'en party is what we want
Dunking for apples must be played.
We love to carve faces in a pumpkin
Look, a spooky lantern, that's what I made.

At the end of this fun day
All we can do is eat and eat
My friends and I are really tired
We collapse into bed, dead beat.

Steven Park (11)
Ballymena Academy

Seasons

Chilly winter wind,
A deserted, frozen pond,
Snowstorm like white foam.

Spring has now arrived,
Buds will begin to blossom,
New life like sunrise.

Summer has begun,
Holidaymakers travel,
As birds migrate.

Fall, leaves turn amber,
Dancing in the storm,
As in a beautiful ballroom.

Chris McDowell (12)
Ballymena Academy

Hunting

Howling hounds waiting to go,
Clipping of hooves,
And the laughter of men and women riders.

As we move off, the houndsman sounds his horn,
Horses prance and dance as they trot up the road.
Finally we get to the field
And both hounds and horses take off.

The heavy hooves of the horses
Pounding through ploughed fields and hurdling over jumps,
And as we near the end of the hunt,
The howling hounds howl no more
And the horses hang their heads low.

We are all glad to be home,
But as always, we look forward to next week.

Ellen Macfarlane (11)
Ballymena Academy

Do Not Spit!

There once was a boy who liked to spit
There was nothing he could not hit
Then one day his mum said, 'Don't spit on the floor,'
So he started to spit on the door

He spat and spat all day long
Even on a guy called Shaun
He phoned the police
They looked at his fleece
Then they started to puke and roll on the ground

While the boy was on the run
He was still having fun
Spitting on shop windows he passed
He tripped and was caught
And he vowed never to spit again.

Philip Jones (12)
Ballymena Academy

The Dentist

The dentist scares me
I have to admit.
In the waiting room
Anxiously I sit.
When my name is called,
In fear I walk in
And he smiles at me
With an evil grin.
'I've a tooth to extract
whether you like it or not -
I'm sure you don't want
Your teeth to rot . . .
If you want to avoid
Looking like a circus clown
Come back next month to get a crown!'

Leigh Kinnear (12)
Ballymena Academy

Orange

What is orange?
Orange is a cat
Striped and fat
And the boing of a ball
Hitting the wall.
A bowl of jelly
Wibbly and wobbly
And the glow at sunset.
It's the tang of soup
And the zing of juice
The smiles of marigolds
And star-like lilies.
It's the signal to get ready
And holding steady.

Katharine Gregg (11)
Ballymena Academy

Darkness

Swallows up everything,
Bird, beast and tree,
One enormous blanket,
Kills laughter, joy and glee.

Under hills,
Behind stars,
Fills up holes,
Blots out Mars.

Devours everything,
Masks all,
Every living thing,
Great and small.

Only one thing,
That can resist,
The sun shining bright,
What a wonderful gift!

John Alexander (13)
Ballymena Academy

My Pony

My pony's name is Crackers
He sometimes drives me quackers
When we go jumping
My blood starts pumping
It's time for my round
The best so far had only one down
I race for the jumps to a great big cheer
I don't believe it, I've only gone clear
First or last, I don't really care
For the best thing about it
Is just being there.

Stephanie French (12)
Ballymena Academy

My Mum

She's like a comfy recliner where you have a nap,
A soft, cuddly piece of fur at your feet,
Her birthday is in April, so that's her month,
As cool as an Afro hairstyle,
As pretty as a purple lily, just blooming,
As sweet as Coke fresh from the fridge,
As energetic as a new BMW.
She's just like a warm jumper, soft and comfy,
She's in her best mood at 5pm,
Just like a tiger who can flare up,
A shiny, new trainer who can jump so high,
A furry cat purring as the evening goes on,
A chocolatey Hobnob in her own little way,
As soft and crispy as fresh oven chips,
As soft and warm as a cold husky dog.

Kelly McCloy (11)
Ballymena Academy

Hurt

Hurt is anger deep down inside,
Hurt is something no one can hide,
Hurt breaks into the tenderest places,
A secret in your heart?

Hurt is spoken through a selfish mouth,
The words they pierce through the skin,
It's the worst form of bullying.

No one can hide if hurt is in their mind,
A real smile will never appear on their face.

They feel alone, no matter how many are around,
Desperate, even though they have everything,
In despair for something, anything,
All to remove the emptiness which the words of hatred
Have left on their hearts, hurt which will never be forgotten.

Amy Alexander (13)
Ballymena Academy

Love

Love is fantastic,
Love is great,
Love is the stuff that makes us date.

It makes you do crazy things
And makes you feel like you have wings.
It makes you feel sky high
And life never seems to pass you by.

You want to look your best,
Better than all the rest,
For the girl who makes you float,
Like you're on a romantic love boat.

Love is amazing,
Love is a rush,
Love is the stuff that makes us blush.

So I'll stop right there,
Before I dare,
To tell you of who's my love,
But she's as gorgeous as a dove.

Robert Barr (13)
Ballymena Academy

Simile About Ellie Bailey

She is as cool as a cat, ready to pounce.
She is as comfy as a chair made out of silk.
She is as bright as the sun on an August evening.
She strikes back as lightning does to thunder.
She speaks as quickly as the wind blows.
She is as cold as a snowman on a winter's morning.
Her voice is as soft as a flute in an orchestra.
She is as loud as an earthquake ready to erupt.

Chesney Bailey (12)
Ballymena Academy

The Keeper

I'm standing here between these posts
And looking up the pitch,
I'm glad I don't have to run up there,
I'm sure I'd get a stitch!

The action's up the other end,
I think they're going to score,
I hope they don't come back down here,
I daren't let in any more!

Oh no, I think I spoke too soon,
That striker's coming here.
There's not one thing that I can do -
Listen to them cheer!

I think I'll try another game,
This job's too much for me,
But what else is such an easy touch?
I'll have to wait and see!

Matthew Houston (14)
Ballymena Academy

Golf

Approaching the first tee,
You come to have a relaxing round,
You hit your first shot,
Disappointment and frustration appear on your face,
The ball only travels seven yards,
You arrive at the ball again,
You swing back,
And smack your second 200 yards down the fairway,
You come to your ball once more,
You take the same swing,
But to your amazement,
Miss the ball completely.
This is going to be another hit-and-miss round of golf.

Alex Simpson (12)
Ballymena Academy

Wind

Many are in fear of me,
Many more are trying to tame me.
My gusts can tear apart a city,
Oh dear, that's such a pity.

Sometimes I'm a gentle breeze,
That means you can walk with ease.
I could perhaps be a twister,
Then I'll blow away your sister.

Sometimes I'm a hurricane,
That's when they will choose a name.
I could be Harry, Sally, Mike or Bob,
I could take away your job.

Why are you so scared of me?
You treat me like the enemy,
I'm harmless, that's what you can't see.
I can't help all the things I do,
That's why I'm much less harmful than you.

Mark Gillen (13)
Ballymena Academy

Autumn

The leaves are turning orange, red and brown,
In the autumn breeze they are gently falling down.
The hedges in the garden have been trimmed up nice and neat,
The only problem now is the leaves are lying at our feet.

Dad goes into the garden shed and comes out with a rake,
I run into the garden - that's a big mistake.
He asks me to help him get some bags from the shed,
I tell him I would rather play football instead.

He tells me to gather the leaves into piles on the grass,
But they blow all over the place every time a car does pass.
At last the job is finished; the lawn looks nice and neat,
If the autumn breeze blows tonight, I will admit defeat.

Peter McNeill (13)
Ballymena Academy

A New Broom

Hey my lad, ho my lad
Here's your new broom
Heaven's your house top
And Earth is your room

Tuck up your sleeves
There's plenty to do
Look at the muddle
That's waiting for you

Dust in the corners
And dirt on the floor
Cobwebs still clinging
To the window and door

Hey my lad, ho my lad
Nimble and keen
Here's your new broom my lad
See you sweep clean.

Daniel McIlhagga (13)
Ballymena Academy

Sweets

Sweets, sweets, sweets,
Who can hate sweets?
The flavours, the types,
Sweets make the world go round.

Sweets, sweets, sweets,
Or what about chocolate?
There's Galaxy and caramel,
That only cost a pound.

Sweets, sweets, sweets,
Teeth rotting sweets,
Like Haribo and Rowntrees,
And the world still turns round.

Jordan Boyle (12)
Ballymena Academy

Autumn

A morning in the autumn
Red shadows on the cloud
The sun hovers low in the sky
Mist, a swirling eerie shroud.

The golden fields in autumn
Grain ripened by the sun
Producing flour for home-made bread
Enjoyed by everyone.

A forest in the autumn
Crisp leaves crunching underfoot
And as if in a distant land,
I hear a car horn hoot.

The ripening fruit in the autumn
Plump, juicy and sweet
Pumpkins, blackberries and apples,
All luscious and appetizing to eat.

An afternoon in the autumn
A blazing sun, but no heat
A chill breeze cuts to my bones,
I rush home to a hot berry treat.

A sky in the autumn
Bright blue with the sun hung low
Then deepening to velvet blue
With the moon and stars aglow.

An evening in the autumn
A soft, scarlet twilight
A cold, sharp bite in the air
Heralds the frost of tonight.

All the sights, sounds, smells, tastes and feelings
Make autumn champion of the seasons.

Helen McKelvey (11)
Ballymena Academy

The Horrible Hospital

Sickly green corridors
And yellowy beds
A hard, musty pillow
Behind every head

The doctors are scary
The nurses all stare
Especially the matron
The one with grey hair

Her piggy, black eyes
Bulge out of her head
There are more than two people
At one of the beds!

'Excuse me,' she grunts
Trying hard not to shout
'Two people per bed, please
Kindly *get out!'*

This hospital's scary
It makes me feel sick
I want to get out soon
Please take me home quick!

Gemma Dennison (13)
Ballymena Academy

Mothers

Do the dishes!
Wash the floor!
Clean the bathroom!
Open your door!

Why must you shout?
Don't you dare say that to me!
It's so not fair . . .
It's a '15' film I want to see.

Walk the dog!
Answer the phone!
Do your homework!
Incessant drone.

You're not going out,
You'll stay here at home,
You can't be trusted
On your own.

We're mother and daughter,
Don't you see?
This is just how
Things are meant to be.

Mary Ward (12)
Ballymena Academy

Our Planet

The Earth is spinning,
Spiralling out of control.
Each day we see the cost,
Pollution taking its toll.

The sea level is rising,
The forests are gone,
The rivers are filthy,
We have been warned.

The ozone is failing
And storms are rife,
But what can we do,
In our everyday life?

Leave the car at home,
Recycle, reuse,
Act thoughtfully for our planet,
Which we can't afford to lose.

Amy McKay (11)
Ballymena Academy

Little Brothers

If they're young, they'll bite,
If they're older, they'll fight.
I'm such a lucky boy -
I've one of each, what a joy!

But James, I'm glad to say,
Will play football and games all day.
And Owen is a child prodigy,
Not in music or art, but in comedy!

So I think when all is said and done,
Without them I'd have little fun.
I really am a lucky boy,
I've two great brothers, what a joy!

Adam Johnston (11)
Ballymena Academy

My Little Sister

Do I have a little sister?
Yes, but thankfully just the one.
She very often makes me wish,
I were an only son!

She really is a terror,
She bites, she kicks, she screams,
She gets away with everything,
Or so to me it seems.

She has a mouth like a gateway,
Well, at least when she's telling on me.
She can tell a tale at least as tall
As a giant redwood tree!

But she'll always be my sister,
And no worse than the others I've seen.
Do you have a little sister?
Then you'll know just what I mean.

Jacob Gray (11)
Ballymena Academy

My Marine Monster

It has to have:
The head of a dolphin,
But the teeth of a shark,
The shock of an electric eel
And the flexibility of a conger eel!

It has to have:
The tail of a humped back whale,
With the body of a killer whale,
The colours of a tropical fish
And the fins of a goldfish!

Mark Lightbody (11)
Ballymena Academy

Daydream

The teacher thinks I'm listening
But I'm really . . .
Playing football at the Nou Camp
With Thierry Henry, Ronaldinho and Pelé

The teacher thinks I'm writing a poem
But I'm really . . .
Travelling to Mars
With Neil Armstrong

The teacher thinks I'm reading
But I'm really . . .
Fighting against
Lennox Lewis, Mike Tyson, Frank Bruno and Mohammed Ali.

The teacher thinks I'm doing sums
But I'm really . . .
Swimming with great white sharks
At the Great Barrier Reef

The teacher thinks I'm writing a story
But I'm really . . .
Tackling Jonny Wilkinson
Stopping him scoring a try against Ireland.

Pete Storey (11)
Ballymena Academy

My Weird New Names!

My name is 'leave me alone'
Don't keep pestering me.
Sports are all I care about,
Not documentaries on TV!

My name is 'I don't care'
Why bother to tidy my room?
It'll never stay clean, not even for a day!
So who cares if it's the bedroom of doom?

My name is 'I haven't got time'
There are 101 things I must do!
Homework, training and practising my flute,
And not forgetting my hated chores too.

My name is 'give it a rest'
You can't criticise me forever!
My homework is fine, the teachers don't comment,
You have to admit, I'm quite clever!

And who do you think you are?
Telling me that I should worry!
My life's going great, so please go away,
Or my new name will be 'you'll be sorry'!

Karla Small (11)
Ballymena Academy

Teacher

We all file quietly into the room
Deep in thought, awaiting our doom -
Our English teacher is new too
She smiles and we're no longer blue.

Advice on giving a talk, first grabs the attention
Of those in the room - 'Don't forget to mention
All relevant points; you have to fully prepare,
Be confident, smile and be audience-aware.'

Drama, poetry, comprehension -
None of these cause us any tension.
Have a clear structure, that's what we're told,
Be enthusiastic, then there'll be no need to scold!

Our teacher makes learning so much fun
Her energy must come from the sun.
We've never liked English this much before -
We're even asking if we can have some more!

Suzanne Dickey (11)
Ballymena Academy

Fun

Fun, the one word that makes me quiver
When I hear the word I just start to shiver
Even if it's just a kite
I'll have fun getting it to full height.

Fun is great to have
When I hear the word I just start to jump about
I start to yell and shout
I just get so excited.

I love having fun by riding my bike
Extreme sport is what I like
Now that my poem is done
I think you will know, I just like to have fun.

Christopher Smyth (12)
Ballymena Academy

Autumn

The blooms are falling off the flowers,
Branches of trees blow with great powers.
The leaves turn gold,
The weather turns cold
And winter is just around the corner.

The field mice search for a safe place to stay,
The cats are having fun, night and day.
Soon cows from the fields will come in,
To be fed with silage and nuts from the bin
And winter is just around the corner.

Eight weeks into the term,
The school children's thoughts excitedly turn
To their Hallowe'en break
And lots of freshly baked apple cake.
Sparklers and bonfires for all to enjoy,
Time to relax for each girl and boy
And winter is just around the corner.

Grace Kennedy (12)
Ballymena Academy

Maybe Some Day

Maybe some day when I'm older
I'll do something to take the weight off their shoulders.

Maybe some day when my school days have ended,
I'll do something good for a violent world, to mend it.

Maybe some day I'll do something great
To end world poverty and all the hate.

Maybe some day when life isn't so fast,
I can take time out and make each second last.

Maybe some day will never come . . .
Help me live each day as if it were that 'some day'.

Louise Shaw (11)
Ballymena Academy

Another Day, Another School!

Crowds of people, big and small,
So many unfamiliar faces.
Corridors and stairs,
Leading this way and that -
Everyone knows this place but me!

A hum of voices,
Excitedly exchanging stories,
Instructions and advice flowing
From a host of new teachers.
Will I ever remember it all?

A smell of disinfectant,
Chemicals and fumes from the labs
And now and again a little waft -
Something pleasant is cooking,
These will guide me through the maze!

A feeling of apprehension flows over me.
My tummy's jittery with nerves.
Everyone has a kind smile,
Making sure we know our way -
Maybe this will be easier than I imagined!

I'm nearly looking forward to tomorrow!

Lois Forsythe (11)
Ballymena Academy

Snowboarding

Wintertime is here once more,
I hope snowboarding isn't too sore.
We're fitted for our boards and gear,
Tomorrow's the day to have no fear.
As darkness descends upon the slopes,
We go to bed full of hopes.

T-bar lifts are not much fun,
Especially when you're on your bum.
Almost at the top, I bounce and hop,
Then everything suddenly comes to a stop.
I've fallen with three metres to go,
As others watch the comedy show.

Eventually I make it to the top,
But when I see the height, I wish I'd not.
Tiny kids go whizzing past,
Showing me it's easy to grasp.
I fall at every single turn,
When am I ever going to learn?

Determined to try once again,
I will succeed, but who knows when?
The snow is soft to cushion my fall,
I must perfect the turn, that's all!
Eventually I find the technique,
What a truly exhilarating week.

Paul Hicklin (13)
Ballymena Academy

The Foxes

As first light dawned
The family came out to play.
Mum, Dad and three little ones,
Crept out to meet the day.

The cubs wrestled in fun,
They tumbled and tossed,
While Mum and Dad watched,
To make sure none were lost.

Too soon they finished playing,
The parents called them to their side,
Something had startled them
And made them want to hide.

With bushy tails and sleek, red coats,
They disappeared back into their den
To sleep another day away
And then to play again.

Amy Hamill (13)
Ballymena Academy

Molly

My pony, Molly, is as cheeky as can be,
She likes to buck and muck about
And then she's full of glee.
Molly is as fat as a barrel
And won't do any work.
But Molly has another thing coming,
She's going to get plenty of exercise
And will not be as fat to look at with our eyes.

Rachel Smyth (11)
Ballymena Academy

Perilous Times

Wind speeds quicken,
Sea temperatures rise,
Storm paths are shifting before our eyes,
Meteorologists know,
Will be certain a storm,
A tropical cyclone has just been born.

Force five was the warning for all to take heed,
Disarray as drivers disperse at speed.
'We're trapped in this city!' the people did cry,
'There's no way out now, the fuel pumps are dry!
We will board up the windows and wait for a bus,
And when all else fails, in God we will trust.'

Abandoned homes,
Food stores are gone,
Hurricane Katrina has come and gone.
Death and destruction she left in her path,
The American flag now flies at half mast.

Melissa McMullan (12)
Ballymena Academy

The Sea In Autumn

Its rolling waves silently lap the shore,
Whilst a delicate mist covers the sea like a soft blanket.
When the calm water lies still,
Its surface gleams in the hazy, autumn light.

When the wispy clouds mask the sun's golden rays,
The cool, swirling sea breeze rides over the waves.
As the breeze becomes a wind,
It brushes the curling crest of each falling wave.

As the sun sets on a beautiful evening,
The sea silently swallows the disappearing sun.
When the full moon is out at night,
A shimmering, silver shadow streams over the sleeping sea.

Rachael Lightbody (13)
Ballymena Academy

The Intruder

Last Thursday night was foggy,
And the air was very still,
As I made my way up silently,
To the mansion on the hill.

I crept so softly round the back,
When suddenly the light came on,
And there before my very eyes,
Was standing Willie John!

I turned and saw a drainpipe,
Curling up the wall,
I climbed in through a window,
Landing in the hall!

I crept into his bedroom,
And there beside the wall,
Lay a pair of dirty trainers,
And a big brown rugby ball.

I crept into the kitchen,
And there lay on the table,
Treasure, which I grabbed and ran,
Back to my home in the stable.

It had been quite a challenge,
Finding cheese in Willie's house,
And very, very tiring,
For me, a little mouse!

Emily McClean (12)
Ballymena Academy

Dottie V Ginger - The Ultimate Face Off!

Dottie:
That annoying little kitten is back!
I thought I got rid of her,
She doesn't get the message,
This is *my* territory.

Ginger:
I have every right to be here,
That old codger's wrong,
She should just step aside
And put me in charge.

Dottie:
Just because she's younger,
Doesn't mean that she's the best.
Didn't her mum ever tell her,
Respect your elders - I'm the boss!

Ginger:
She doesn't stand a chance . . .
What's this?
She actually can hiss,
As if I'm scared of her!

Dottie:
She growls back, doesn't she know?
Experience always wins.
I've been in more fights,
Than she could ever be in.

Ginger:
I'm strong, I'm fast,
And she's just too old!
She leaps at me,
Ouch! My ear!

Dottie:
That will teach her.
She's run away!
But I know she'll be back . . .
Some day!

Georgina Collie (11)
Ballymena Academy

To The Circus

When I enter the tent of joy,
The music blares all around,
Like playing a guitar with a drum,
It's the sound of the circus!

As they bring in the animals,
Led by a tall, greenish clown,
I turn my eyes
And give a frown.

The acrobats jumped
And the audience cheered,
But some of their positions,
Were totally weird!

Filled with laughter by the end,
I was quite glad I came.
But the question that ate at me . . .
Was it good or was it bad?

Gary McKendry (12)
Ballymena Academy

A Snake

A snake is a wonderful creature,
Its skin is sleek and shiny,
But rough to touch and feel.

A snake is a beautiful creature,
Its flickering tongue is slimy,
But sensitive and natural.

A snake is a strange creature,
It sheds its skin when growing,
But looks fresher when it's done.

A snake is an old, old creature,
Because it's been here for some time,
But when it's got to go, it will leave us all behind.

Jonathan McBride (13)
Ballymena Academy

The Portrush Raft Race

Along the prom on a summer's day
Crowds of people have gathered.
It's the raft race today
And everyone is excited.

Colourful rafts are lined along the beach
Blue, pink, red and yellow.
Competitors are ready with oars in hand
The klaxon sounds and they're off.

Crews enter the roaring sea
The air is filled with cheering and laughter.
Now the hard work begins
To see who will finish the race.

The weather gets worse, it's cold and windy.
Some rafts are sinking
Others drift towards the rocks.
Now the spectators start to get worried.

The lifeguards help those in trouble
To bring some back to dry land again.
The air is now filled with worried gasps
Hoping that no one has been hurt.

A few complete the course into the harbour
Only five rafts out of about fifty-five.
The winners shout and cheer
They probably can't believe they have won.

The race is now over,
People seem tired and relieved.
Money has been raised for the lifeboat
I'm going home now to build my raft.

Rachel Keys (11)
Ballymena Academy

Perfect Poppy

Perfect Poppy,
Loved to copy,
Other people's work.
She would sit beside Bart,
Who is really smart
And cheat, cheat, cheat.

As the day went by,
Her teacher asked why,
She had the same answers as Bart.
She said she did not study,
For she went out with her buddy
And didn't want to get a low mark.

Her teacher was cross with Poppy,
Especially when she got all soppy.
So don't cheat,
Sit in a seat
And get your books out to study.

Nicole Bradley (11)
Ballymena Academy

My Little Brother

He is like the month of December
He is crispy and white like snow
He is like the season of winter
Which is cold and cool
He is like a wardrobe
He's strong and broad
He is like a big lion
He is fierce and is the king
He is like a Saturday morning
He is frosty and fresh
He is like a Ferrari
Which is fast and furious.

Peter Gillespie (11)
Ballymena Academy

My Sporty Family

This is my family,
We're a rowdy lot,
One thing's for sure,
Couch potatoes, *we are not!*

My mum, she likes to swim,
It really clears her head,
She gets up very early,
Instead of lying in bed!

My dad loves to play golf,
But it won't make him rich,
The ball is seldom in the hole,
But often in the ditch!

My sister she plays hockey,
It's her favourite game,
Hopefully when she's older,
It will bring her fame!

Well me, I like them all,
Rugby, football, cricket,
Because in my mind,
They are all so wicked!

Then there's my dog Bonnie,
She loves to go out for her walk,
She is my furry friend,
I just wish she could talk!

So that's my family,
And all the sports they play,
That's what keeps us busy,
Through every single day!

Jonathan Dinsmore (11)
Ballymena Academy

Sunday Breakfast

In the kitchen lots of food
All tasting good

Smell the sausages, sizzling in the pan
Hear the whizzing, of the fan

Eggs, bacon and the bread
Good to eat after bed

Table laid out from the night before
Oops
Mum drops an egg on the kitchen floor

Children come streaming through the door
Sleepy faces, ruffled hair, fighting over chairs

Once the food is served, no noise can be heard
Just satisfied faces, all in their places

Everyone full up, weighing a ton
Running away one by one, to have some fun

All that is left are the dishes
How Mum wishes . . .
For help with those dishes!

Rebecca Smyth (11)
Ballymena Academy

The Hockey Final

The feeling of dread when I wake
The not hungry but have to eat feeling
The pre-match butterflies in my stomach
The everlasting car journey.

The age to find the team
Everyone silent
The tense, robotic warm-ups
The not listening to the team talk.

The getting into places in slow motion
The century before the whistle
It finally comes
The we're off!

The pass-back to me
The lightning zigzag passes up the pitch
I'm in the box, just the goalkeeper and me
My heart stops, *help!*

The *clack* as I rocket the ball into the goal
The roar of the crowd
The feeling inside, *glory, honour, pride*
The *win!*

Hannah Stevens (12)
Ballymena Academy

The Needy And The Greedy

Sometimes we really don't think
How very lucky we are
We always have plenty of food and drink
And get driven round in a car

Many people in countries afar
Have to look in bins for food
They don't even know what phones are
And some live in huts made of wood

We get clothes all the time
Even when we don't need them
And we even have the cheek to whine
When we don't get our chosen item

So now it's time to have a thought
For people who live in misery each day
Be more grateful for what we've got
And give what we can to people far away

So when you go to buy something nice
Remember my little verse
It's the needy not the greedy
Who need to be thought of first.

Jade Frew (12)
Ballymena Academy

Elephants

Elmer is an elephant,
Multicoloured is she,
She's had lots of adventures,
Big and brave is she.

My favourite animal is an elephant,
You must wonder why I like them.
I'm not sure why I like them,
But I just do.

Some elephants have big ears, others don't,
They've got a long trunk, but a very small tail,
Their legs are thick and they are very tall,
But their ears keep them cool.

Some elephants are killed just for their ivory,
Which I think is really cruel,
It should be banned, not done at all,
Would you like it to be done to you?

I wonder what it would be like to be an elephant,
Swimming in a crystal clear pool,
Having a handy water pistol,
To soak you through and through.

Rachel Dunlop (12)
Ballymena Academy

Winter's Back

Winter days are coming fast,
Chilly days and dew on grass,
Summer days have been and passed,
Christmas is coming soon at last!

Children playing in the snow,
Carol singers in a row,
Street lamps give a little glow,
Dark, cold days go very slow.

Turkey on the Christmas table,
Children in bed being told a fable,
Lots of food sat on our tables,
Surely more than those unable.

Robins are out and flying around,
Ice on the road and very slippery ground,
But the true meaning of Christmas I hope you have found,
Jesus, our Lord, was sleeping sound.

Opening presents on Christmas Day,
Having so much fun, the day flies away,
Children inside with toys for play,
Then out comes the pudding on a fireproof tray!

Laura Barron (11)
Ballymena Academy

My Gran

My gran is the best gran the world's ever seen,
She always was the dancing queen,
She dances and prances all day long,
Listening to the same old song!

When my granda comes home,
He just wants to sleep,
But that's a hard job,
Listening to Gran's beat.

The music's turned up,
Neighbours get cross,
Babies just cry,
While Gran makes some pie.

When I go to Gran's house,
I don't know what to do!
She sings and she dances,
Even with a brew.

What would you do if you had a gran like mine?
For my gran even prances before she will dine!
So this is the end of my story,
And to Gran we'll give all the glory!

Edward Wilson (12)
Ballymena Academy

The Ancient Mummy

Deep in the deserts of Egypt
There lay a dead mummy
Some explorers set out, not one was a dummy,
With their swords equipped.

They set out for the legendary gold
That lay by the mummy's coffin
And according to some boffin,
It looked to be really old.

As they entered the pyramid,
One of the explorers was bitten,
As the ancient book had written,
Mosquitoes in the pyramid were amid.

They finally reached the ancient tomb
And there the gold lay,
But the mummy had vanished away
And was not in the room.

The mummy tapped the explorer's back
And Immediately devoured him.
Soon gone were the rest of them
And nothing was left but a rucksack.

Conor Swain (12)
Ballymena Academy

Seasons

The greatly anticipated season of spring,
The buds are beginning to show on the tree,
They soon will all burst open,
The bright yellow daffodil is free!

Long, hot, glorious days of summer,
What a joy to feel the sun on our back.
Adults and children alike love the carefree days,
Laze about, have barbies on the deck!

The gentle, golden mists of autumn,
Sweep across field, forest and hill,
We begin to wrap ourselves in warmth,
Not wanting to freeze in the chill!

The last season of the year,
Though not to say the least.
We celebrate the festival of Christmas,
When families join and enjoy a feast!

Seasons come and seasons go,
We enjoy them all, in good times and strife,
We admire and applaud them all,
In the great circle of life!

Catherine Dinsmore (13)
Ballymena Academy

The Experiment

As I gaze through the science door lab,
I see a man dressed in white,
Giving orders, 'Bunsen burners on!'

When I enter the room,
Unburnt gas fills the air,
Bunsen burners roar and the hot blue flames leap into the air.

Students wearing goggles, carefully weigh
Crystals as green as grass,
An experiment is about to begin!

Test tubes rattle, taps *drip, drip, drip,*
Water bubbles like mad as the Bunsen burner does its job.

Green crystals turn brown,
Smoke rises like a snake into the air
And suddenly, a crack of thunder fills the room.

The teacher shouts,
The students scurry,
Bunsens are extinquished.

The experiment had an unexpected ending!

Ashley Hamill (12)
Ballymena Academy

Autumn

Autumn is the time of year,
When harvest time and Hallowe'en appear.
Wind and rain and cold, bracing weather,
Long gone are the days of buttercups and heather.

The coloured leaves fall all around
And reds and yellows flood the ground.
Sycamore and old elder tree,
A wonderful scene of great beauty.

From underneath bushes, hedgehogs appear,
Then scuttle away and hide in fear
And rustle around in twigs and leaves,
Then amongst the roots of trees they weave.

Shorter days and longer nights,
The eerie darkness gives you a fright.
Morning fog turns the blue sky grey,
Farmers' barns burst with bales of hay.

November comes and winter is near,
Songs from the robin birds we can hear.
Autumn is over, cold weather to come,
The favourite season has ended for some.

Emma Wray (13)
Ballymena Academy

Winter Again

Winter again, how I hate to see it come,
When it gets all cold and wet,
I love to get hugged by my mum,
Where does all the bad weather come from?

How I hate winter, the fog and the rain,
Wishing I was back on holiday in Spain,
The dark mornings and nights,
Wasting electricity by turning on the lights.

My mum she loves winter,
The crisp, cold, fresh air,
Warm coats and jumpers,
Make it easy knowing what to wear.

So my mum thinks winter is a cool season,
She says it is lovely and pretty,
And so that is my reason;
I still hate winter, when the ground gets all slippy.

Nicolle Scroggie (11)
Ballymena Academy

Hockey

It's Saturday morning, time to get up
I get out of my bed with a moan.
Into the bathroom, a quick wash then I go
As I get ready I groan.

It's off to school with my mum in the car
I think it's going to rain.
I'm off to play hockey with the girls in my year
I think it's a bit of a pain.

I could be lying in bed, nice and warm
Instead of being out in the cold,
But now on the pitch I'm playing a game
I'm only doing what I've been told.

The time soon passes, it's time to go home
I see my mum from afar.
She's coming to take me to shop in the town
She'll soon be here in the car.

Victoria Bond (11)
Ballymena Academy

Make Poverty History

M alnourished children
A re dying. Terrible diseases are
K illing millions
E very year.

P eople in Africa deserve the gift
O f life that we have.
V olunteers have been sent over to aid but
E very three seconds one mother's child still dies of poverty.
R ebuilding the lives of
T he destitute is a hard task, but
Y ou can hear crying babies in the distance.

H ear the cries of starving and
I ll-fated Africans.
S top the poverty in the
T hird World
O r more deaths and disease will come.
R ead this poem and please remember that
Y *ou* can help to change this.

Craig Simms (11)
Ballymena Academy

Colour

Red, blue, orange, yellow and green,
There are many colours to be seen.
Hundreds and hundreds of shades of each,
From fluorescent orange to soft, pale peach.

Neon green and orange, fluorescent yellow too,
Then there are the pastels, soft pink and baby-blue.
Everyone has a favourite colour, you know what you like,
Everything is that shade, from your T-shirts to your bike.

On your bedroom walls and in your locker tight,
Are colours of every shade, some are dull, some are bright.
You use them at school and at home every day,
We all use colour in every possible way.

The world would be very dull, without any colour in sight,
Nothing would be bright and cheery, just simple black and white.
I'm glad we all have colour, on our streets and in our food,
Wouldn't you be sad without all the colour? I would!

Jenalee Kennedy (13)
Ballymena Academy

His Choice

Her day began just like yesterday
Bright mood, new clothes, lots of plans.
For him, it was a day unlike all others he had lived,
Dark elation, baggy clothes, no earthly future in his mind.
She met her friends and joined in the fun,
While he made his last journey alone.
Her jokes and laughter were unending,
But his silent mind was focused on his task ahead.
Without ever knowing her,
He chose to change her life forever,
As he ended his own.
She was walking along the street when, *bang!*
In drowning terror, but senses alert,
She sees for the very first time,
A scene that changed her views forever.
Death, destruction, devastation, desperation,
Screaming, wailing and pleading appeals,
Smoke, blood, helpless victims, squirming on the ground,
Corpses and unspeakable horror everywhere she looked.
Fear, mixed with impending doom engulfed her,
As the wailing sirens arrived,
With help and hope for the survivors,
But no hope at all for him.
He made the choice . . . she paid the consequence.

Conor McMeekin (13)
Ballymena Academy

Christmas

Busy is the shopping mall,
Shelves no longer stacked so tall,
People queuing everywhere,
Shop displays now left bare.

Towns covered in colourful lights,
Illuminate the now dark nights,
Decorations swamp the trees,
Presents piled up to your knees.

A thick, white blanket covers the ground,
Crunching feet are the only sound,
Skaters spin across the lake,
The Christmas spirit is now awake.

The work has all been done,
Anticipation has begun,
Milk and carrots by the fire,
Children start to tire.

Early they wake,
No sound do they make,
Disbelief in their eyes,
All around paper lies.

Happy faces can be seen,
Where the magic sleigh has been,
Asleep are Santa and his deer,
Until this time next year.

Matthew Hanna (12)
Ballymena Academy

The Headless Horseman

His body rides through the night,
Alone on his horse he gives you a fright.
A pumpkin has replaced his head
And when it falls off, he's still not dead.

Some people say he comes out on Hallowe'en,
But I believe it's only on Friday the 13th.
I see his body once every year,
And on that night I'm full of fear.

He has no real eyes, mouth or nose,
But in that pumpkin it all shows.
Down in the graveyard is where he haunts,
And children believe he has fun when he taunts.

His name was always full of fame,
Of course it was Brian Candalain.
He haunts every year because of this,
He's visiting his family and so much does he miss.

All of this is really true,
About the horseman through and through.

Naomi Bell (12)
Ballymena Academy

The Rainforest

The scary snake slips and slithers slowly beside the small stream,
silently stalking the scrumptious squirrel.

In the small stream beside the scary snake
and the scrumptious squirrel,
furious fish are fighting ferociously for the food floating among them.

Next to the scary snake, the scrumptious squirrel, the small stream
and the ferocious, fighting fish,
worms are wiggling wildly, without warning of the hefty hawks
hovering above, harassing the hopelessly helpless worms
underneath.

Near to the scary snake, scrumptious squirrel, small stream,
furious fish, wiggling worms and hefty hovering hawks,
giant gorillas grasp for bananas whilst annoying apes
arouse asleep animals with their annoying noises.

Not far from the scary snake, scrumptious squirrel, small stream,
furious fish, wriggling worms, hefty hawks, grasping gorillas
and annoying apes, sawing sounds can be heard,
and all the trees are disappearing one by one,
making all these creatures disappear as well.

Jonathan Gordon (14)
Ballymena Academy

The Night Sky

The day is gone,
The sun is down,
The street lights are on,
Where there is no one around.

Up above you raise your eyes,
Dusty grey clouds,
The moon so high,
A crescent shape but almost round.

A clear black blanket,
Flickering lights,
Sparkling bright diamonds caught in a net,
On a windy night.

Through the night the sky slowly moves,
The clouds cover the moon,
This poem I don't have to prove,
The night will show itself soon.

Aoife Kennedy (12)
Ballymena Academy

Fairies

Full of sparkle and colour,
They fly around each other.
Dancing in the light,
From morning to night.

Their wings shine,
Like a silver dime.
With a twinkle in their eyes,
While they play with the flies.

With tiny hands and feet,
Everything is very neat.
Stripes of silver on their wands,
Their hawthorn tree is near the pond.

Each of them is very different,
Colours change from blue to mint.
Rainbow jewels on their clothes,
Glitter from head to toe.

Catherine Mark (12)
Ballymena Academy

Life

Life can make me feel
As happy as can be
But sometimes in life this
Just cannot be me.

Life is sometimes cruel
As painful as death
It can be unfair
And as angry as fire.

Life can often be
As fast as a rocket
Often it gets too fast
And I get whisked away.

Then sometimes life is
As slow as a tractor
And I fade away
Until I laugh again.

I shout and I scream
As loud as a steam train
But still I don't get
My own way in life.

I wish life could be
As peaceful as a lake
On a calm summer's day
I could sail away.

Sarah Hamill (14)
Ballymena Academy

The Shadow

He follows me
Everywhere
I can't escape
He knows my every move
Like tree roots to the ground
He clings onto me
He can't jump
That's your only escape
Being airborne
But you can't stay up there
Forever
You have to come down
Eventually
And then you're stuck again
Like glue
He's on my tail
From dawn till dusk
But no earlier
No later
For he has one weakness
That comes around every twelve hours
Give or take
Such a simple weakness
The night
He needs light to survive
And there's none of that at all
At night
My only escape
From the one that they call
The Shadow.

Charles Deane (14)
Ballymena Academy

Terror

Way up above, a plane does fly,
Hidden against a darkened sky.
But something else soars up so high,
While on your window seat you sigh.

You try to rest, drown out all light,
But a glimpse of fear gives you a fright.
You jolt up straight, you stare at the night,
But nothing is there in plain sight.

As paranoia takes its place,
You quickly glance the time to race.
You peek outside at an ugly face,
Coming towards you at full pace.

A hook rips through the metal floor,
Of a creature you see more.
A wing, a tail and wounds of war,
A great eye with an evil core.

A dragon, now the creature's name,
An impossible beast to tame.
Acts like a child, playing a game,
Loops around, for its mouth to aim.

It breathes its fire and then a sigh,
It comes to you, you start to cry.
Your tears well up, but instantly dry,
You realise that you're going to die.

The floor collapses as you weep,
Consciousness you cannot keep.
You fall into a dreamless sleep
And tumble down to a sea so deep.

David Nesbitt (13)
Ballymena Academy

The Battle Of The January Sale

Their eyes were glazed, their jaws were set,
Their faces gaunt and grim,
Their feet march on, relentlessly,
They chant their chilling hymn.

'Bargains!' is their war cry,
'No quarter!' their lament;
The tears of joy drip down their face,
'Down thirty-five per cent!'

'Reductions!' is their mantra,
As they stampede through the store,
The weak are trampled underfoot,
And squashed upon the floor.

One raises her umbrella high,
To strike a granny down;
The granny parries with her bag,
And thumps her on the crown.

They dive upon the clothes racks,
It's survival of the fit,
The small are decimated,
By the screaming mob for credit.

At last it all is over,
And the bodies cleared away,
The warriors back to the mundane,
Dull life of day to day.

But say 'bargains' to the housewife,
Watching strong men blanch and turn pale,
At the gleam of blood-lust in her eye
From the January sale.

Hannah Drennan (14)
Ballymena Academy

The Cup Final

Out of the changing rooms
The players emerge
To a standing ovation
From the on-looking crowd
Everyone's nervous
For the day has arrived
When two teams will battle
For the coveted prize.
The whistle blows
And the match begins
The atmosphere's tense
For who will win
Both teams have chances
But no team scores
As the game approaches
The half-time break.
The players return refreshed
With renewed confidence
That their team will win
And hoist high the Cup.
Into the net
In the blink of an eye
The ball thunders
Out of the goalkeeper's reach.
The fans are jubilant
The game is won
The whistle announces the game is done!

Timothy Scott (12)
Ballymena Academy

Bullying

Bullying is wicked
It does no good
It is very sad when
The victim isn't understood

It is trying, it is depressing
It sometimes ends in death
It is often started meagrely
And grows to something big

The worse tool used
Is *your* silence
It is used in many ways
So talk

You really need to speak
To someone who
Is able to deal with it
In a short time

Bullying takes many forms
So don't be confused
Many types are known
And all can be sorted

There are many people
To help *you*
If only you would tell them
What is happening

It is time it was stamped out
For good.

James Simpson (14)
Ballymena Academy

The Ugly Duckling

All sense of life and happiness left her.
Her face tingled as the blood slowly dripped between her eyes.
The class cackled like the witch who created that bitter-sweet apple.
Her hands fumbled as she wiped away a hot tear.
Her features were plain and boring
She never forgot.
She was short with a dumpy figure
It haunted her day and night
She was called 'the fat' or 'the ugly'.
She resorted to measures unhealthy
To get rid of the feeling of numb.
These left her more miserable than before
As her sins tormented her to insanity.

Then she met this guy who called her a name.
A name she had never been called.
He called her beautiful.
He wanted to be her friend.
She was confused. She didn't understand.
How could someone lie so cruelly?
He said, 'I love you'
Then showed her how much.
He accepted her . . . and after a while
She believed.
Then one day she discovered something radical.
She had friends.
She was still plain with a dumpy figure
But she forgave herself for the past
And inside found a beautiful swan
There was no reason to fear.
People have feelings. Accept it.

Pippa Kirk (16)
Ballymena Academy

The Jump

I know I shouldn't be doing this
But nobody's really looking
And it's not my fault
The temptation is too much to handle
I slip outside
Yes, my partner in crime is there
A quick greeting, but then down to business
Rock, paper, scissors
I have to go first
Of course I'm excited, yet my heart is pounding
I'm not an expert, but I can do it
I grip the wall, like a mountaineer doing his job
What if I fall?
I don't think about it, my focus is on the task
I stand on the wall, looking down
It's not that big a fall
I'm ready for it, and have been these days of planning
The person inside my stomach is somersaulting
No more thoughts, just jump
And so I do.
For a second I'm floating, like a man on the moon
But then I crash down to Earth
The trampoline is damp, my feet slip
I close my eyes and slowly feel the water penetrating
Through the back of my thin T-shirt.
I've done it.
So I didn't land very well
But like I said, I'm not an expert.

Ruth Campbell (14)
Ballymena Academy

Poems

Poems can have really, really long lines
That seem to go on forever and ever,
Or short ones.

They can be in a uniform
Like a bunch of school kids in French class,
Or free verse like when they come out of school.

You get poems that rhyme
All the time,
Or never, not even once.

Some use metaphors or similes
Some use onomatopoeic words
Some use made up words, but somehow we still know what they mean
And some don't use any of these
And leave it up to your own imagination.

Poems can build wonderful pictures of rainbows, castles
                                                  and unicorns
But they can also build up pictures of your deepest,
            darkest nightmare, slowly creeping into reality.

I like poems.
Poems that rhyme.
Poems that make me laugh.
Poems that make me weep.

But most of all, I like poems that I write myself.

Emily Stewart (13)
Ballymena Academy

Love

Sometimes I wonder
If people love me
If they care
Or am I dreaming?

If they love me
Why do I get the feeling
That I am in a world of my own
Like my head is in the clouds?

Their love means a lot to me
But if they don't show it
What's the point of feeling love
When you don't show it and then it is wasted?

So if you love someone
Show them just how much you love them
If you don't, you don't realise how much love you are wasting.

Gemma Scott (12)
Ballymena Academy

Breaking

Wanting to talk, but
Having to watch from afar
For now we mustn't exist.
Our love has a bar.

We walk past in corridors.
She is nobody special.
In reality to my existence;
She is crucial.

We will have to wait for a while
With the clock ticking,
And in all that lonely time
My heart will be breaking.

Conúil Duffy (17)
Belfast Royal Academy

Dead Men

Dead men don't talk,
Dead men don't walk,
Dead men don't do anything,
But you still can't hide from their sting.

Wherever you are,
They're always there,
Wherever you go,
They're trying to steal away your soul.

Their memories haunt you,
Whatever you do,
You can't change what you never had,
Even though you feel so bad.

Dead men don't talk,
Dead men don't walk,
But what you never had the chance to say,
Will haunt you till your dying day.

Amber MacLennan (15)
Belfast Royal Academy

She Was Gone

In the twilight, she walked alone
And tried to get away
She pitied every blade of grass
For planted it would stay

But by the time the morning came
She was no longer there
There was no trace she left behind
Not a single strand of hair

We asked a lot of people
But they simply couldn't tell
But someone who had seen it
Said the story played out well

When everyone was still asleep
She was the only one
She just let go of all she held
And she was gone.

Alannah Clarke (12)
Belfast Royal Academy

The Battle

(Inspired by 'The Siege of Helm's Deep' from JRR Tolkein's masterpiece
'The Lord of the Rings: The Two Towers')

The defenders stood upon the battlements,
As the bitterly cold wind
Viciously bit their freezing flesh.

Rain plummeted down on each man,
As the attackers marched toward
Their doomed foes.

Each defender stood resolute
As they looked at this huge, barbaric force,
The feeling was not of fear,
But uncertainty.

The attackers, siege weapons at the ready,
Were prepared for war.
This was the last obstruction in their way
And as they vastly outnumbered their adversaries,
They were confident.

Blood would be spilt,
Lives lost,
But one thing
Would not be extinguished
On either side,
Pride.

And as the moon shone,
The first shot was fired,
And the battle had begun.

Steven Laverty (15)
Belfast Royal Academy

I Wanna

I wanna be a star
I wanna go far
I wanna drive
Around in a big red car

I wanna sing
I want some bling
I want my song
To be a mobile ring

I wanna be top
Work non-stop
I wanna know rap
And even hip hop

I wanna dance
I wanna prance
I wanna jump about
With a guy called Lance

I wanna be a star
I wanna go far
If only I could drive
A big red car.

Fiona Henderson (12)
Belfast Royal Academy

Why?

Why is the world a circle?
Why is the grass green?
Why is the sky blue?
Why are there people?
Why are there houses?
Why were we created?
Why is the sea blue?
Why is the sand yellow?
Why are we all different?
Why does it rain?
Why is there snow?
Why is it sometimes sunny?
Why is it windy?
Why is it warm and cold?
Why are we black and white?
Why are there cars?
Why bikes?
Why, why, why, why? Oh tell me why.

Aaron Rush (13)
Christian Brothers' School

Blue

Blue is a summer day sky,
Blue is an island ocean,
Blue is a blueberry pie,
Blue is the ink from my pen.

Blue is the coldness in winter,
Blue is the lightning,
Blue is the colour of my eyes,
Blue is blue mould on bread.

Blue is a sapphire diamond,
Blue is the colour of bubble gum juice,
Blue is the colour of a metallic blue car.

Colm Grego (13)
Christian Brothers' School

Sports Analysis

Football is a good sport
The manager gives his team a talk
The players walk out
They're lining out on the pitch
From keeper to striker
In a giant stadium
The ref blows his whistle
The Hoops are piling pressure
Then comes the goal!

Tennis is a good sport
The players come out
The packed-out stadium gives a loud shout
The umpire waves his flag
They take their rackets out
He gives the ball a whack
The ref shouts out.

Boxing is a good sport
It's very rough and tough
The ref rings the bell
He comes in - upper cut
And it's a knockout.

Darragh Byrne (13)
Christian Brothers' School

Colour - Haiku

Green is the nice grass,
Orange is the lovely sun,
Blue is the deep sea.

Gavin Lavelle (13)
Christian Brothers' School

Celtic Forever

My team's from Glasgow
Wearing green and white
They're sponsored by Nike
And by the fans they're liked.

I get up early to catch the bus
To bring us to the docks to get the boat
The fans are singing loud and hard
'Come on the bhoys play with heart.'

Outside Celtic Park
My hands are shaking
Because we play Rangers
The win's there for the taking

I take my seat
It's a fantastic view
Rangers come out
The crowd's cheering, 'Boo.'

Kick off!
Celtic have possession
Give it to Nakamura
He puts the ball in the back of the net!

Lennon goes down
Thompson steps up
Curls it in sweetly
The Celts are two-nil up.

The match is over
Celebrations all around
Next week
I'll step into the exact same ground.

Gerard Hanna (13)
Christian Brothers' School

Violence

Many people nowadays don't even care
About what's in the world no more, about what's even there.
The thing that I really hate in this world today is violence,
People being killed and suffering in silence.

The worst thing thugs do is shoot people with a gun,
Yet I seem to fail to understand how they find it fun.
Thugs don't understand it and I think they never will,
That it's not fun, nor legal, to just go out and kill.

If you want a good life, and a good job too,
Then don't kill, go to school and do good the whole way through.
The one thing I don't get is why they kill again,
Do they understand what it's like? Do they not know the pain?

But still violence affects us all,
Even if it is small.
Now violence happens here and wherever,
I wish it would stop forever and ever.

Colm Bellew (14)
Christian Brothers' School

Blue, Blue, Blue

Blue is the colour of sea and sky
Blue is the colour of many's eye
Blue is my favourite colour, you ask why?
Blue is the colour that I see day and night.

The *b* is for beautiful
The *l* is for luxury
The *u* is for unique
The *e* is for elegant

Because blue is like no other colour.

Rudy Van Merkom (13)
Christian Brothers' School

Man Of The Future

I am a child.
I am all the things of my past.
The hair of my mother,
The eyes of my father,
The hair of my small brother,
The look of my biggest brother,
The size of my middle brother,
The width of my sister.

I am all I see.
I see my mum in the morning,
I see my dad in the morning.
I am all I hear.
I hear cars every morning,
I hear church bells every Sunday.

I love my mum.
I love my dad.
I hate Burger King.
I hate watching golf.
    One day I will be an adult.

Michael Rice (14)
Christian Brothers' School

Why?

Why do trees grow so high?
Why does life pass us by?
Why can I not touch the sky?
Why did my dog die?
Why can fish swim so fast?
Why must we live on land?
Why can we not jump up and fly?
Why do mountains stretch so high?
Why does the Earth have to be round?
Why do we have to die?

Christopher Giliroy (12)
Christian Brothers' School

Colours

Red is the colour of my blood
Green is the colour of my eyes
White is the colour of my bones
Blue is the colour of the sky.

Orange is the colour of the sun
Brown is the colour of trees
Black is the colour of the ground
And gold is too precious to be sold.

Grey is the colour of my school jumper
Yellow is the colour of my tie
And when the sun goes down
Pink comes into the sky.

Conor Carnahan
Christian Brothers' School

The Match

The manager roars as the ball comes in,
The overhead kick goes straight in.

The crowd rage at the referee's decision,
The strikers are playing in the wrong position.

The free kick is curled around the wall,
But unfortunately it's not the right ball.

The pass from the defender goes astray,
That I think wasn't good play.

The match ended in a two-nil win,
That performance needs to go in the bin.

Ryan Lewsley (13)
Christian Brothers' School

Disasters!

Why are there disasters all over the world?
Why are there hurricanes which barge through our towns?
Why are there tsunamis which wash away our lives?
Why are there earthquakes which bring everything down?
Why do we have floods which make us move out?
Why do we have poverty, no money, no jobs and no lives?
Why can't we all live the same?
Why?

Why do we have war
Killing our fellow people, our friends and our families?
Is it to prove we are better than others? Why?
Why do we have paramilitaries with their guns and their bombs
Destroying our communities, our families and our lives?
Sectarianism destroys all our lives, our football, our rugby
and all the rest of our sports.
So why do we have it?
Why do we have terrorists blowing up our world,
killing thousands of people?
Why do we have suicide bombers killing themselves?
Is it for revenge? No one knows.
All those thoughts are running through my head
and I don't know *why!*

Liam McAughey (14)
Christian Brothers' School

Colours

Red is like an apple
Orange is like the sun
Blue is like the sky
Just like my eyes
Green is like the trees in the springtime
White is like the clouds in the summertime
Unlike some days where the clouds are grey
Like the colour of the roots.

Sean Tolan (13)
Christian Brothers' School

Wartime Regrets

The random beat of exploding bombs,
The smell of sweat and decay,
The sight of hundreds dead and decaying,
The squeaks of hundreds of rats,
The screams of pain as men die,
As loud as a banshee's cry,
The memories of these horrors,
Will haunt my dreams,
Until the day I die,
Come home as an amputee,
With scarred memories,
My life has changed for the worse,
The only thing left to do . . .
End my retched life.

John Hollywood (15)
Methodist College

Bang! Dead!

The horrible sound of bombs and guns,
Echoed through our heads,
The painful memories of what we'd done,
Would forever be beside our beds.
They knew nothing, did nothing and deserved nothing,
But that's the way it was in war.
We watched their loved ones weep at the sight,
Their innocent relatives massacred.
'For what?' they said.
'It was the training inside our heads!' we said.
It was then I put a gun to my head,
Bang! Dead!

Nick Kirkwood (15)
Methodist College

Freedom?

Genocide, massacre,
Excruciating pain,
What's this for?
Who here will gain?

War is hell,
They refuse to see,
They don't care about anyone,
Even little old me.

The war is over,
But not for me,
The memory lives on,
The agony I still see.

I left a proud soldier,
I left a proud son,
Look at me now,
The damage is done.

I cannot sleep,
My head is my cell,
I spend my days,
Still living in hell.

I sit here now,
Gun to my head,
Soon it'll be over,
Soon I'll be dead.

Michael Fletcher (15)
Methodist College

My Poem

I will never forget that day
The day when sin was released from Hell
We rushed along the water like a sea of torpedoes
Men praying to see their families again
Others throwing up whatever food they had in them
We could hear the soldiers in front, landing on the shore.

Then we landed on the shore, there was gunfire everywhere
You could hear the screams over the top of the explosions
Men were jumping off the side to avoid the German machine guns
So over I went, so scared I could hear my teeth chatter.

Then in the water there was a sort of peace from it all
Until men began to panic, giving us away
Shots moved slowly through the water
As I watched them tear through the bodies of my fellow soldiers
Then having to watch their lifeless corpses float to the top
It soon turned into a graveyard of men in a pool of blood.

Once we had made it up the beach
The sand had turned red from countless deaths
With enemy machine gunfire pinning us down
We rose to the challenge and advanced
Then the guns were ours and within only minutes
The beach had been taken
All the men cheered for glory
But deep in our souls we knew we had witnessed Armageddon.

Sam McCune (16)
Methodist College

Darkness

Darkness surrounds my consciousness
Receding into the infinity
My confusion evident

Flashes of the past
Weaving through my mind
Impossibility a reality

Pain, cracks through my hand
Pulling away in disgust
From the shuddering edge
That reaches for my flesh

A sharp dig
Release from anxiety
A drip, a splash
An end.

Ngozi Anyadike-Danes (14)
Methodist College

I Lie Silently . . .

I'm not crying but there are tears hiding behind my eyes,
I'm not bleeding but the pain is killing me inside.
I'm not listening but every word is going through my head,
I'm not speaking but there is so much more that needs to be said.
And undeniably I'm hiding behind a made-up wall,
I don't want to be a hero because I'm afraid that I will fall.
People wonder why I question but words don't leave my mouth,
I lie silently and watch as my world slowly falls south.

Morgan MacIntyre (13)
Methodist College

What I Hear When Viewers Come To See My House

It scares me at times
When I hear a shuffle of feet in my house,
A silent stillness of people looking,
Heavy breathing, the sound, soft sound
When my mum shows them around.
In each room their facial expressions
Almost make a sound,
The realtor is standing in the distance
Slurping, sucking at his tea.
He makes hissing noises as if something was wrong
When he was evaluating the house.
The people stomp off and say,
'We'll get back to you'
And their car drives off.

Jayne McCourt (14)
Methodist College

Invisible

I stand still in the corner of the street,
Voices are muted, seeming far away.
He doesn't see me as I freeze in mid sentence,
He never does . . . but maybe today?

We used to laugh as friends together,
But now that's all in the past.
A chill, a tear runs through me now,
It all went by too fast.

I'm lonely now as he talks with her,
My soul is slowly tearing.
My breath is snatched, full of sorrow,
For you love, I feel nowt but caring.

Christina Bennington (13)
Methodist College

Will She Be Found?

They burst in the door
Fighting the flames
Searching the rooms

The alarms, they sound,
But will she be found?

Look, in the bedroom!
Sprint up the stairs
But no she isn't there.

The alarms, they sound,
But will she be found?

Then, what's that?
They hear a scream
Will it be too late?

The alarms they sound
But will she be found?

It's gonna blow!
Boom! it's gone
The house, it fell down.

She lay on the ground,
And was never found.

Debbie Neely (13)
Methodist College

I Hear . . .

When I think of the train
I hear . . .
It pulling into the station
People shuffling towards the doors
The *pishhhh* of the doors opening
People hurrying to get a seat
The thud of bags being thrown onto the rack
There is almost silence
Apart from the chattering of schoolchildren
And the scenery whizzing by
The faint sound of the conductor's dull voice
The rustling in pockets
Searching for tickets
When I think of the train
I see . . .
Less graffiti than on the older ones
The rush to get off the train
People searching for tickets
The conductor punching holes
The crowd at the station
Waiting for a train or bus
Crowds shuffling to the train
To start their journey again.

Rory Tinman (13)
Methodist College

A Child's Pain

Why hit a child if it doesn't work?
Why hit a child if it breaks your heart?
You have to stay strong.
Your child will only take it for so long!

Ever looked in your child's eyes,
But can't stand it when she cries?
Why does your child cry for so long?
Maybe the pain has hurt for too long.

Your child starts to do wrong and,
What do you do?
Keep beating the child,
Making sure the pain goes on and on!

Years go by.
As your child says goodbye,
You say you're 'sorry'.
But her tears have gone dry.

The pain stays with your child
For all those times it was too wild.
She thinks about it every night
And so with you, it's regret and fright.

Your child has her own one,
You say, 'Treat them right, not wrong!'
She just smiles and walks away,
As she remembers the pain of another day.

So walk away and say goodbye,
But don't forget,
She'll not turn back.

Just know why!

JulieAnn Courtney (16)
Our Lady of Mercy